GROWING UP WITH GHOSTS

Silver City, Idaho, in the 1890s.

GROWING UP WITH GHOSTS

MEMORIES OF SILVER CITY, IDAHO

Julia Conway Welch

Library of Congress Catalog Card Number 84-091394

Lithographed and bound in the United States of America by
The CAXTON PRINTERS, Ltd.
Caldwell, Idaho

DEDICATION

IN MEMORY OF
ELIZABETH BLAKE CONWAY, 1877-1948
&
PATRICK CHRISTOPHER CONWAY, 1870 (?)-1958

TABLE OF CONTENTS

LIST OF ILLUSTRATIONS

GROWING UP WITH GHOSTS
INTRODUCTION

Visiting the scenes of one's childhood, either the physical act or taking the trip by way of memory, can lead to surprises and disappointments. A television newsman lamented just the other day the passing of a secret place where he and other children had reveled in the privacy of a boulder-strewn wood. When he went back to see it, he found the place paved over, built up, obliterated. Urbanization hasn't touched the town I grew up in and its natural beauty has been enhanced by the passing years. Since its long mining career has virtually ended, the trees and shrubs on the mountainsides, no longer needed for building, fuel, and mining operations, have returned to the pristine state when it was an Indian hunting ground. But the town itself has suffered many changes. Its last period of prosperity in the 1890s extended on into the first years of the twentieth century. My memories of Silvery City, Idaho, begin after the last boom, during a period when there was a false boom because of World War I. After the War mining was sporadic, poorly financed, and temporary. Businesses closed, people moved away. The town was on its way to becoming a ghost town.

When I began recalling those years I became aware of two influences in our lives. One was the effect of the town's isolation — a factor that posed great problems at times but at other times compelled us to draw on our own resources for entertainment and distraction. Another was the fact that the town's past was its time of glory, that the present was often discouraging and the future doubtful. We tended to take comfort from the past and to live on false hopes of its repeating itself.

The geography of this corner of Idaho south of the Snake River is one factor responsible for its isolation. It is less than seventy miles from some of the valley towns but steep foothills and deep canyons lie between the river and the mountains. Such problems in road engineering are easily solved today but at considerable expense. In this case the road would not go anywhere except to Silver City — a dead-end in the Owyhee Mountains. At the very time such roads were being built for the convenience of gas driven vehicles, Silver City's gold and silver production came to an end erasing any economic reason for a good road. Another reason for its isolation is climate. Storm tracks from the south and west carry moisture in the form of snow to these high mountains isolating them in some years as late as June. The expense of keeping such a road open would be out of the question for a large, poor, sparsely inhabited county like Owyhee.

A phrase I frequently heard as a child was "in the early days." Those were the times of the fabulous gold strikes, of great demand for miners, of high wages, and exciting happenings. The old timers laughed now at their former hardships — the cold, the jerry-built shacks they lived in, the long hours and hazardous conditions in the mines. There were many invidious comparisons between "then" and "now." For many of us who were growing up at the time, the past we heard so much about was an era of wonder and excitement, and when we heard some of the old timers say confidently about the town "Oh, it'll come back," we believed that the whole colorful panorama of the early days could repeat itself. Later when we had to leave this place, it was hard to adjust to the towns in the valley whose ideals were progress and the future.

I call this account of life in a dying town "Growing Up With Ghosts" because of the influence of the past on our lives. It is the story of one family, seen through the eyes of one of its members rather than a chronicle of the whole town. I haven't created incidents, but at times I have dramatized them. Any attempt to recall the past involves a certain amount of creation. Events do not happen in words: words are the tools to make them live. I have tried to make this memoir real enough so that its readers would have the feel of life in a dying town in the early years of the twentieth century.

GROWING UP WITH GHOSTS

CHAPTER I

TOWNS ALONG A CREEK

My sister and I came home from playing at a friend's house one day in 1917 and announced that our friend's mother had seen a ghost. She had not only seen it peeking out from behind the tattered curtains of the old War Eagle Hotel but she knew its name. It was, she told us, the ghost of Kate Blackinger, a seventeen year old girl who had died there in "the early days," as the past was called in our town. The family we were visiting that day had been thousands of miles away at the time Kate died. They had, in fact, arrived from Ireland less than twenty years ago and had brought with them a great supply of Irish imagination which the mother had combined with the local story of Kate to make an interesting tale.

I was six and my sister was eight and at our ages we believed nearly everything we heard. On our way home we stopped briefly in front of the old Hotel — its very appearance was enough to encourage belief in a sighting — to study the ragged lace curtains from a safe distance across the road. We were eager to see a ghost, but afraid, too, that we might.

We were surprised at the reaction our news produced at home.

"What nonsense!" My mother said indignantly. And she added a few hot words about people taking advantage of children.

My father put on a thoughtful look as he often did when he wanted to make fun of us.

"Now I wonder," he mused, "where she could have got hold of a bottle."

Perhaps he was only half joking, for these were Prohibition days and the problem of finding alcoholic beverages was acute. Anyone suspected of hoarding a bottle could be sure to have many friendly callers.

A few days before, our friend's mother had been lamenting to Mamma that her youngest child — a boy of five — was about to celebrate his birthday and "there was not a drop in the house." Maybe Daddy was wondering if she'd had a bit of luck.

I don't know whether on this occasion he treated us to one of his sermonettes on the Irish people, but it certainly would have been a fine opportunity. The Irish, he often said, were the most ignorant, the most backward, the most superstitious, people on the face of the earth. He knew about them first-hand for he had been born and spent his early years in County Kerry, Ireland. He had escaped the plague himself by becoming a student of geology and a disciple of Bob Ingersoll, a nineteenth century evangelistic agnostic, casting out not only superstition but his religion as well.

The rebuff we received at home didn't have a great deal of effect on our gullibility. We went on believing pretty much what suited us. There was a steep, narrow, passage between buildings in our town which was known as "Dead Man's Alley" because three violent deaths had occurred there. We didn't know the stories of the unfortunate incidents but the name suggested to us that we might see something exciting in it. So we often took the alley instead of the prosaic road to give ourselves a thrill. After we learned our parents' attitudes on the subject of ghosts our trips up and down the alley couldn't be mentioned at home for fear of ridicule.

Courtesy of the University Press of Idaho, Moscow, Idaho
Schoolhouse, hotel, and bunkhouse, Delamar, Idaho, 1936.

We lived in a town that was becoming a ghost town, but that romantic term had not yet been applied to it: to us, it was just a town with a lot of empty houses and other buildings, and these, instead of pointing out the direction in which it was heading, became just another source of entertainment. We would press our noses against the glass of abandoned enterprises to study a background scene left behind by a photographer or a saloon's silver ceiling. Sometimes when we found the door of an empty house ajar we went in and looked around and tried to imagine ourselves living there.

We had moved to this town from another mining town nine miles down the creek where Sister and I were born and where my mother and father met in 1908. Delamar, named for its founder Captain Joseph De Lamar, a nineteenth century financier, was a company town; that is to say, it owed its existence to a single company, a single mine. And when the mine ran out of ore the town died. Many of its buildings dated from the 1890's when the wealthy captain sold the mine to an English company for two million dollars. The second owners built a new hotel to replace one which had burned and added other new buildings. When the mine closed in 1914 and nearly all the miners left town, Delamar was in much better physical shape than the town we moved to — Silver City, an older settlement and one that had been experiencing ups and downs since 1865. *It* was not a company town. The mountains rising from the bed of Jordan Creek, the town's uneven site, supported several mines, and although no great discoveries had been made recently and most of them were managing to stay afloat by selling stock to the credulous on the basis of the region's fabulous past, at least there was a chance here for a hard-rock miner like my father to find work.

He was working for the English company in Delamar when he met my mother who had come to the town to visit a sister whose husband was running a general store. How their meeting and subsequent engagement took place I've never heard. But I know her marriage was a surprise to her family who lived in Boise at the time. After Mamma went back to Boise her older sister went to Delamar to take her turn at visiting. This sister lived with their widowed mother and had come to think of herself as the "boss" of the family. Mamma didn't confide her plans for marriage in her, probably, I think, because she might have decided to put a stop to it.

While the older sister was visiting in Delamar the priest from Boise came into town to say Mass and, since there was no Church in town, my Aunt Jennie, the Delamar resident, invited him to hold services in her house. On being introduced to Miss Reby Blake, the older sister, he said: "Oh, yes, I married your sister Elizabeth in Boise yesterday." When Aunt Jennie told me this story many years later she said with great emphasis: "Well, *Reby* had a *fit!*" If she had known some of the traits of my father's character her reaction might have been worse.

Mamma's family was Irish on both sides and Roman Catholic, although her father, Tomkins Blake, a Dubliner, was a convert from the Anglican Church. Her mother was born in my father's home County — Kerry. It was the kind of match that a computer, having been fed these simple facts, might have given its blessing to. But the Blakes belonged to a different social class. Mamma's brothers and brother-in-law worked for merchants in Boise and later became merchants themselves. They belonged to the up-and-coming business element of the young state of Idaho. Daddy considered himself a "workin' stiff," and was a member of the miner's union. He was proud of his physical strength and his popularity in these rough little mining towns where a person who was a "character" was a special favorite. His stentorian voice, his merry ways, his love of jokes and odd sayings, his enthusiasm for dancing and a night out with the boys, endeared him to many. Mamma was quiet and shy: she didn't dance and she didn't make friends easily. And she worried about the future — especially after we were born — while Daddy went on blithely enjoying the present.

One of the traits that might have worried Mamma's family was that he was so hooked on prospecting that he would walk away from a good job any day to try his hand at a promising quartz vein or a likely bit of placer ground. He had abandoned his original trade — saddle and harness making — when, on his way west from Missouri, he heard some lectures at the University of Wyoming on mining and geology. It was a turning point in his life. He never seriously practiced his trade again although he made a few saddles for some cowboy friends in Owyhee County, the huge Idaho county about one-third the size of Ireland, with Silver City as its county seat.

The first winter of their marriage my father succumbed to the

Elizabeth Blake Conway

Patrick Christoper Conway

prospecting craze and carried Mamma off to a cabin on the far side of Florida Mountain where they stayed, snowed in, until spring, while Daddy satisfied himself that there was after all no rich vein in an old mine. This was her introduction to his cavalier attitude toward money and the future.

They came back to Delamar in the spring and he got a job in the mine and another one as well. When the Company had a load of gold and silver bars or bullion, ready to be hauled to the railroad, it kept their departure secret for fear of hold-ups. The man who drove the team and wagon over the steep mountains needed another man with him to spell him with driving and guard the load in case of trouble. He needed a strong man who was good with horses; my father fitted the bill perfectly. He had worked at different times driving teams for the livery stables in town and he was well-known for his skill with horses. So, my mother remembered, they would be awakened at odd hours, Daddy would get dressed, and they would quietly sneak out of town. I often wondered when she told about these trips how on earth his partner managed to keep him quiet until they got away, for if he wasn't talking in his powerful voice he was always whistling or singing.

I was too young when we left Delamar to have any memories of the town. I remember it from the times we visited or passed through it after we moved to Silver, when the silent buildings and the empty streets gave me the impression that something awful had happened here — not just the closing of the mine, but some tragedy which had caused its abandonment. I know from the stories I heard about it that it must have once been a very lively place. The gulch of Jordan Creek was narrower there than Silver's and it had to accommodate the huge dump of the mine, the mine buildings — a mill, assay office, and mine offices, a bunk house, and the handsome hotel the English company had built. There were houses on the steep sides of the gulch (which was more like a canyon than a gulch) and a neat little brick schoolhouse with a belfry and a steeple. There was not much building room along the creek after these places were accommodated, so at a spot beyond where the canyon narrowed and then widened again, another part of the town grew up. The one with the mill and mine was called "Upper Town" and the other "Lower Town." The latter was lower not only in the sense that it was farther down the creek: it was lower in that here some of the baser wants of the populace were suppled. Its nickname was "Tough Town." Saloons, Chinese gambling houses, even opium dens, and a house of prostitution existed alongside perfectly respectable businesses, livery stables, and homes.

Aunt Jennie, whose husband's store was in Tough Town, liked to recall a day when the doctor had gone to Jordan Valley, Oregon. While he was gone three members of the community died unexpectedly: a baby died of what might have been sudden infant death syndrome, a young woman in the house of prostitution who had been ailing died suddenly, and a young man, a handsome fellow, according to my aunt, died in the arms of his companions as they were walking him along the street to combat an overdose of opium. The doctor had to be summoned back from Oregon but he arrived too late to administer to any of his patients.

That was not a typical day in Tough Town, of course, but it gives some indication of how it got its name. The house of prostitution was operated by a woman named Jennie Mitchell who had moved her business from Hailey, Idaho, when the Wood River mines closed down. Her house was not far from the store my uncle kept and, from old pictures of it, it looked like other houses along the street, with a neat front yard and a picket fence. Some of the sporty fellows in town sometimes had their pictures taken in front of the house with some of the girls. The madam was apparently careful about her image in town. At Christmas time she gave every child a gift. When my sister and I were christened in 1909 and 1911 she presented our parents with a five dollar gold piece.

It must have seemed to the people of this prosperous little town that they would spend most of their lives there, for the mine had produced millions for the English company as it had for Captain De Lamar. Two hundred or so men were employed by the mine and the mill. Counting the families of the men and the people who provided services for the town I suppose its population must have been seven or eight hundred. Many of the miners were from Cornwall, England, where they had learned their trade in the tin mines. They were known here as they were in other mining towns from Minnesota to California as "Cousin Jacks." I've heard that the name originated because when another miner was needed in the mines some Cornishman always had a cousin Jack he could send for. They brought with them their odd manner of speaking and the terms they had used in the mines in Cornwall. Some of these became a part of the language of Western mining, and they furnished the dialogue of "Cornish" jokes. These jokes were not necessarily derogatory. They made fun of the quaint terms of speech rather than the man himself, for these miners were acknowledged everywhere from Connecticut to Almaden, California, as experts. Their unfluence in Delamar extended beyond the mines to the kitchens of the town. When miners in a drift sat down together at what the Cornish called "crowst time" and opened their "tommy tins" or dinner pails, the delicious aroma of the Cornish pastie — a meat-and-vegetable filled pastry — inspired many a non-Cornish miner to demand that his wife learn the art of making it. It was enjoyed hot from the oven at home or cold in the mine. And storekeepers in town stocked plenty of black tea, and saffron for another Cornish specialty — saffron cake.

Other nationalities were represented in Delamar, too. Charlie Forni, who ran a livery stable, was an affable Italian whose jokes were quoted in town. My father worked for him at one time and they became very close friends. There were several Irish families. One very sociable old lady named Mrs. McGeogh was a puzzle to my aunt because, contrary to her sociable reputation, she failed to call on her. When she finally came it was obvious that her call was prompted by the fact that she had heard that my grandmother — another Irish lady — had come to visit her daughter. Her apology for being so remiss became a favorite joke in the Blake family, three of whose members, including this aunt, had married Germans. "I would have come to see you before," she said. "But I thought you were Dutch."

The town of Delamar didn't survive the blow of the mine's closing in 1914. It has been said that the beginning of World War I in Europe was the cause of the English Company's abandonment of its efforts there. But it may have been that the War precipitated a withdrawal that was inevitable. For the veins of ore in this part of the West did not hold up as long as the ones in Virginia City, Nevada, and even those couldn't hold a candle to the biggest gold producer in the United States at Lead, South Dakota.

The town's buildings were torn down slowly over the next twenty-five years. Only a few frail structures mark its site today. The huge dump of the mine and the cemetery above the town give some indication of the life of its past. Many of the stones of those whom the town outlived are cut with loving verses and some of the children's graves have odd wire mesh fences around them with an arch of the same mesh over the top and a hook suspended from it to hang flower baskets on. They look today like rusty baby basinettes. The people who put them up probably thought they would be decorating them with flowers for many a year. But the closing of a mine in a one-mine town scatters its population in all directions and its raucous, bustling, life vanishes like a puff of smoke.

Child's grave in Delamar cemetery.

CHAPTER II

FROM HOUSE TO HOUSE

When we moved up the creek to Silver (we used this shortened version of its name) there was a renter's market on houses, for the town had suffered several mine closures between 1910 and 1914. I don't know how many houses we lived in before we found one that suited our needs and could be heated cheaply. Most of the houses were poorly built. They had been thrown up hastily in good times and allowed to fall apart in poor ones. In spite of the harsh winters, few showed that any care had been taken to shut out the icy blasts. The only insulation from the cold was often that provided by nature: heavy snow sheltered them from the blizzards this country was famous for.

Mike Rock, a character from the early days, was the chief landlord of the town. He bought up houses, contents and all, from their owners as they left to look for work in other mining towns. I have only vague memories of some of the houses we rented from him. I remember one that had an ancient grand piano in the front room, rendering it almost useless as a room. Another house next door to Mike's own, I remember quite well. It had some very odd pieces of furniture (I suppose they would all be precious antiques now) but the strangest of all was the bed Sister and I slept in in the front room. It folded up into a handsome light oak cabinet in the daytime. The front of the cabinet was carved ornately and sported a mirror. Opening up our bed and getting it down at night was an experience we looked forward to, although we were like most children in hating bedtime. However with our handsome bed a part of the living-room decor, we often got to stay up late when we had company.

This house was referred to in town as "the Heidelberger house." Quite a few houses were named after families who had once owned them, or even those who had only rented them, but had somehow left their mark on the community. The practice has survived to this day, and the mark of a real old-timer is that he will correct your naming of a house with a much earlier one. I think the practice originated because there were no house numbers to identify them and, in most cases, no streets for them to be on. Houses were built on the sides of the gulch wherever there was a place that could be made into a building site. Some sites were blasted out of bedrock and others faced a road, street, or trail and were built up in back to accommodate them to a slope of the ground. So the practice of saying "the Heidelberger house, the Rowett house, the Townsend house," became a reliable way of pointing out a house in conversation.

I didn't know who Sam Heidelberger was when we lived in the house named for him, but later I found his grave in the cemetery and read about him in "the Blue Book," a local history published in 1898.[1] The back pages of the book were devoted to pictures and biographies of certain citizens. I think probably those who were included had to buy a number of books, for stacks of them could be found in empty houses. Sam came to Silver in 1866, "with a capital of one Mexican dollar, which he still retains as a pocket piece," the Blue Book says. He had emigrated from Philadelphia to California, to Portland, Oregon, to Boise Basin (another Idaho mining district), and finally to the Owyhees. His was a typical pattern of a man following the gold rushes. Those who were disillusioned with opportunities in California moved up the coast to places like Jacksonville, Oregon, another boom town, then on to Portland and up the Columbia to Idaho. And the overcrowding in Boise Basin sent them on to Silver City, a fresh gold strike. Sam worked as a peddler when he first came to town, and as a printer's devil for the newspaper. He opened his first store in 1872 but went broke after investing in mining stocks. He evidently went into business again for he had another setback in 1876 when many of the mines closed after the panic of '75. The Blue Book describes this second reverse as "severe losses in book accounts," which means that a lot of people left town owing him money. By 1898 he had "worked up to the front rank of merchandising with a large store and varied stock." I don't know whether he built the house we lived in or just lived in it during his prosperous later years. He married in 1879 and that may have been when he built or moved into it.

I started to school when we lived in this house. I can remember walking down the steep hill on a path cut out of the snow. It was more like a tunnel to me because I couldn't see over its snowy sides. That winter was one that caught a lot of moisture from both south and west. My mother decided that the weather was too severe for anyone my age to venture out in, so after Christmas she kept me home. The shift boss at the mine where Daddy worked had made me a small pair of skis and I spent the afternoons out in the drifts behind Sam Heidelberg's house learning to ski. It seems like a contradiction that my mother would keep me home on account of the snow and then let me go out and tumble around in it. I think I must have worn her down by my pleading to use those skis and she finally turned me loose to get some peace.

My trips across town to the schoolhouse on the other side of the creek gave me an idea of the kind of town we lived in. It was all either up or down hill except for a stretch in front of the Courthouse and the general store. And even this street, the main one in town, plunged down hill at one end and up over an extrusion of bedrock at the other. The buildings across the street from the Courthouse were the kind of false-front buildings you see in Western movies. Nearly all of them had recently been saloons. They were built to conform to the slope of

Photo Courtesy of Idaho Historical Society

The power poles in this picture date it as after 1901. The Courthouse is on the left, the saloons on the right.

the land behind them by having an under-pinning of timbers enclosed by boards. These lower areas were used for storage of wood or other items. Some had porches on the back and stairways by which the saloon patrons had easy access to the houses of prostitution on the street below. At the time I became familiar with the town I had no idea what purpose the big houses behind the saloons had served, and the one old lady who still lived there — Old Jo — was just a pleasant old lady with a rather odd name. When she died I was surprised to learn from her obituary in the Avalanche, our newspaper, that she had a real name like everyone else.

The sidewalks along the saloon buildings were wooden, but this year, 1917, the Courthouse was being enlarged in the direction of the general store and a cement sidewalk laid in front of it became the only one the town could boast of.

We crossed the creek on a narrow wooden foot bridge which spanned not only the creek but part of the gulch. It had railings about three feet from its floor and the older children walked on them, balancing themselves with outstretched arms. I'm sure I didn't try this stunt until later, but after we moved to a little house behind the schoolhouse it became one of the rituals we followed when we were sent to town on an errand.

I don't suppose I noticed until some time later the peculiar construction of many of the buildings in town. From a front view they seemed to be one building but when you saw them from the back it was plain that they were really two or three buildings, even four in one case, jammed together, some of one story, some two or three. This construction shows the haste, even the desperation, that went into the making of the town. Some of the structures had been moved up the creek from two other towns, already abandoned in the '60's, and they were hastily united so the owners could begin reaping the business bonanzas of those frantic early days.

Our year in the Heidelberger house was a happy one because the country's participation in World War I brought some prosperity to the mining industry. The need for silver brought entrepreneurs to town to open up some of the old mines where they hoped to find ore that had been passed over in earlier times as not worth the effort. A few new mines followed veins which they hoped would lead to bigger ones. Wages were high during this period: even miners had money to buy War Bonds and Savings Stamps. The town suffered the same shortages that the rest of the country endured. White flour and sugar were rationed. Nearly every housewife made her family's bread, and the use of non-rationed graham and oats called for some adjustments. I can remember the ladies who gathered at each other's houses to work on Red Cross projects, laughing over their failures with the new grains.

The War years brought a lot of sociability to the town. A dance followed by a midnight supper was a popular way to raise money for the bond drives or the Red Cross. They were held in the largest single building in town, the Masonic Hall, which straddled the creek alongside the footbridge. Its hardwood floor provided a good area for dancing, and upstairs there was plenty of room for trestle tables to be set up. These were heavily laden with casseroles, salads, pies and cakes — a veritable "groaning board." People of all ages attended. Children were bedded down on benches along the wall under their parents coats when they became sleepy. My mother usually sat with the older women, talking and watching the dancers. My father enjoyed himself hugely and noisily as he whirled around the room. Round dances with a caller shouting "doise do" and "a la main right and left" involved the whole crowd and we children were allowed to run out on the floor and break into the circle. When the music stopped after one of these gay rounds my father would let out one of his happy howls and set the crowd laughing.

The War was still on when we moved to a house on the main street of the town in 1918. It was owned by one of the pioneer ladies who had moved to a smaller place when her husband died and her children grew up. It was completely furnished with pieces she had collected since her arrival in the territory in 1865. The house was larger than most houses in Silver. It had three bedrooms furnished with old-fashioned bedroom sets which included wash stands with bowls and pitchers. It had two bedrooms on the front of the house divided by a hall which led to the living room and dining room. The third bedroom on the back of the house opened into the kitchen. This house, like so many in town, conformed to the uneven terrain by being built up on a foundation in back. It was unlike many of them in that its foundation was made of stone blocks.

My sister and I slept in the third bedroom off the kitchen. It had a piece of furniture that was even more unique than the folding bed in Mike Rock's house. It was a bath tub which folded up against the wall and looked like a closet when not in use. To take a bath you let it down and filled it from a hose attached to the kitchen sink. It was drained like any bath tub by a pipe that was somehow not affected by lowering or raising it and which exited from the house at the top of the high foundation in back. When my sister and I took a bath we always jumped out quickly after pulling the plug so we could run to the window and see our bath water cascading in an arc toward the lower street.

While we lived in this house so near the business section we became more thoroughly acquainted with day to day events and with the people who played a part in them. Every day but Sunday we went down the street to get the mail from the post office. We got to know the post mistress and her cowboy husband, the stage driver, the telephone operator, the people who ran the stores and the hotel. In the post office people gathered to wait for the mail to be distributed and here we heard the news and gossip of the town.

Because there was no way of knowing just when the stage would arrive we often made more than one trip before our mission was accomplished. During the summer months a big black touring car carried mail and passengers in and out to the railroad at Murphy, Idaho. In the spring and fall when the roads were muddy, horses and wagons took over. In winter sleighs came in over the seven thousand foot summit. Whatever type of vehicle made the trip we always called it "the stage," a hold-over expression from the early days when a real stage coach, which now sat on the lower street by a livery stable, made the trip.

We were like the pioneers in this part of the country in that we regarded the stage as our link to what we called "the outside" — that is, to the settlements in the Boise Valley of Idaho. In spite of the fact that the automobile had greatly shortened the time required to reach our town from the valleys we were still cut off from easy access to them for many months of the year. And the arrival of the stage did more than confirm that we were still in touch with the outside: it gave every day a purpose, an event to look forward to. When, in very bad weather, the stage didn't make it, we went to bed with a feeling that the day hadn't ended properly.

Recently I saw an item on the historical page of the Idaho Daily Statesman from 1882 which points to some of the hazards which occasionally delayed the stage:

"PAXTON IS SAFE: Deputy Marshall Paxton arrived home on Friday night, as sound as ever. He says the storm in which the stage was caught in the Owyhees was the worst he ever saw, and he has seen a few snowstorms. He was alone in the snowbound stage for thirty-six hours without eatables or drinkables, and very sick from an old malady besides."*

Often when we were playing with other children in front of this house we noticed a passerby whose manner was very different from other people in town. Miners and prospectors on their way to War Eagle Mountain would stop to say a few pleasant words or at least give us a friendly greeting. But this man strode by with his eyes fixed on the distance and the stick he carried rapping out measured strides. He did not seem to hear us or see us. Why was he so different from the others who passed? One day an older child who happened to be there told us: the man was a Count. He belonged, according to our informant, to a noble family in Europe who sent him money to work his mine on the side of War Eagle.

When we broke the news of our discovery at the supper table Daddy roared with laughter.

"Count!" he cried. "He ain't no more Count that I am." Then he explained that this poor man was insane and one of his delusions was that he belonged to a noble family in Europe. The name "Count" had been applied to him in derision.

But why, we wanted to know, did our informant tell us that he was really a Count.

My father laid his hand gently on my sister's arm and said tenderly, as if he were speaking to someone almost too infirm to bear the news: "Honey, I'll tell you what: people will believe what they want to believe. And if it's more fun to believe that that poor crazy fellow is a Count, why, that's what they'll believe. But," he leaned over to look her in the eye to emphasize the confidentiality of his disclosure. "You and I know better."

* Reprinted in the Idaho Statesman, Jan. 25, 1982

In spite of the delicate way he handled it we got the point that we had been taken in again.

In the middle of the winter of that year, Andy Swan, a miner who sometimes spent the whole year on his claim, came down to report that, after observing that there was no smoke coming from the Count's stovepipe, he had cautiously crept close enough to look in the window. He saw the old man on his bed surrounded by his guns and knives, apparently dead. Andy's caution was well founded, for the Count suffered from delusions of persecution as well as delusions of grandeur and had threatened to kill anyone who set foot on his claim. The sheriff went back with Andy and confirmed that the man was dead. They found a map in the cabin which marked the spot on his claim where he wanted to be buried. When they came back to town they looked around for volunteers who would be willing to climb the mountain through the heavy snow and help bury the Count according to his wishes. My father agreed to go and made a harness for himself and the others to pull the Count's coffin on a ski-sled. The men wore webs or snowshoes so they wouldn't sink into the heavy drifts. The cabin was just over the top of the mountain on the east side and, once on top, they had to fight wind and snow together. Daddy and Andy knew the mountain in every detail for they had claims just over the top on the west side. Even though visibility was near zero they guided the party in the right direction and found the half-buried cabin. Digging the grave was a monumental task. Ten feet of snow had to be removed first: then with picks and shovels they attacked the hard ground. They admitted when they came back to town that the grave was not deep, but they managed to dig a big boulder out of the snow and roll it on top of it. That big boulder is the Count's uninscribed monument.

His cabin was still there the last time I visited the mountain. It had been robbed of its windows and doors and was just an empty shell. The scene from that spot is magnificent. Hayden's Peak, the highest in the Owyhees, rises in front of it, and the drop into Sinker Creek is precipitous. I hope the old fellow enjoyed it.

On one of our trips to the Post Office during our summer in that house in town we brought home a letter that made Mamma's face light up with joy: her sister Ellen, the only one of the large Blake

The Count's cabin.

View from the Count's cabin.

family who had not migrated to the West, was coming to visit us. She lived in Chicago and she worked at a grand store we had heard much about from Mamma, for she had worked there, too. It was Marshall Fields or, as she and her sister referred to it "Fields." Ready-made clothes were not as available as they are now and many women still picked out material and had their clothes made by dressmakers. That was the kind of work that Mamma and Aunt Ellen did. Because she worked in that store and lived in a big city our aunt was already endowed with a certain glamour. And in addition to that, we had never experienced the thrill of having a visitor in our house. It was lucky that at this time we had a house with an extra bedroom and that the bedroom was furnished with old but respectable furniture. Mamma occupied herself up until the very day of her sister's arrival with cleaning every inch of the house. Sister and I helped but we still had time enough on our hands to make the days drag mercilessly. At last the great day came: she was to arrive on the stage when it got back from Murphy.

We made several trips down the street before noon on the slight chance that the stage might make a record trip. It had to wait for the train to arrive from Nampa with mail and passengers, so there was not much chance of its arrival before noon, but we didn't want to take any chances. After lunch we settled down on a bench on the Hotel porch and watched the bridge at the bottom of the hill. The car finally rumbled over it and ground up the hill. We ran for the Post Office where it would stop first. We had already spied two ladies in the back seat and as they got out of the car we ran to Aunt Ellen and grasped her hands. She stood for a minute talking to the driver who assured her that he would bring her luggage up as soon as he unloaded the mail. We led her off triumphantly before the envious eyes of other children.

She walked slowly in her high heels and she stopped for a moment to look with dismay at the hump of bedrock that rose in front of her as the street assumed a higher level. We were so accustomed to this eccentricity of the main street in town that we scarcely noticed it, but to her it was a real obstacle. We took her hands and steadied her while she found footage on the bulging rocks. I wonder now what she must have thought of this strange little town where no one had ever bothered to level out the streets. When she made it to the top of this little rise she was out of breath. "Wait," she panted, "I want to ask you something: how did you know I was your Auntie when I got out of the car? You came right up to me instead of the other lady." We thought at first she was teasing us and we just laughed instead of answering. But she persisted, asking her question again, until finally I said: "We didn't know you: we knew the other lady." This struck her as terribly funny and she remembered it and told it when any of the relatives came to Chicago to see her for years afterwards.

During the few days of her visit she and Mamma had a lot of catching up to do on all that had happened in the ten years they had been separated. But she paid quite a bit of attention to us. We were fascinated by the care she took of her hands and finger nails and when she offered to use her magic equipment on us we were delighted. She was shocked at the condition of our hands when she set to work on them. We spent much of our time playing in the water of an icy little spring which ran down the hillside in front of the house, damming it up and floating chips of wood in it for ships. The cold water and the rough rocks had reddened and cracked the skin of our hands until they were almost beyond salvage. But after several of her treatments they began to look quite decent. She also undertook to make some changes in our speech. When we answered her in the affirmative we said: "Ye-as?" in the western fashion. She objected to the drawl and also to the way we left the word up in the air as if we were uncertain of ourselves. "Say 'Yes-s-s!'" She'd tell us, hissing the letters out like an angry cat. It was easier to change the looks of our fingernails than it was to alter our speech patterns. We wondered secretly what the other children would think of us if we went around hissing out our yeses. But we tried our best to make the acceptable sounds in her presence.

We were all sad when the stage stopped at our door one morning to take her back to the outside. She had brought some of the glamour of city life to our household and her lady-like ways had made somewhat of an impression on us — more on my sister than on me, I'm afraid, for I was soon playing in the little stream again, and saying "Ye-as?"

All during the summer of 1918 we studied the big black headlines in the Boise paper when we picked it up at the Post Office. The word

"Huns," so convenient for headline writers, struck fear to our hearts as we spelled out the terrible events of those last days of World War I. I did not know why these Huns were so terrible until I saw a picture in a magazine at a friend's house. It showed the Germans with their spiked helmets marching through Belgium; one of them had a baby impaled on his bayonet. After I saw *that*, the Huns figured heavily in my dreams. I wondered if I wouldn't wake up some morning and find that they had crossed the summit and were marching up the street to our house. One night in November I was sure that they had at last penetrated our gulch when I heard gunfire all around our house. I woke my sister who was one of those sound sleepers whom nothing awakens, and we lay there trembling and listening. Then I saw that there was a crack of light under the door that led to the kitchen and I could hear Mamma's and Daddy's voices. When I got up my courage to open the door I threw myself in Daddy's arms and asked if "they" were coming to get us. "Who?" "The Huns!" This set him off into one of his roars of laughter. Sister came out in time to hear the good news that the shooting outside was nothing but Silver's celebration of the end of the War. The news had just reached the town by telephone and everyone who owned a gun turned out to salute the occasion. We all sat around the table in the kitchen and had a cup of tea with canned milk in it.

The next year we made our last move to a little house that was newer and better built than most. I think we were the last tenants in the house on the main street. It was only a few feet from the old War Eagle Hotel which had long been closed and, some time during the next few years, both of them were torn down. All that is left of the house are some of the stones of its high foundation. Sam Heidelberger's house is one of the seventy buildings of the town which has survived. It looks down now from its rocky perch on the ruins of the Courthouse.

CHAPTER III

SETTLING DOWN

One summer not long ago when I was pointing out to a friend on her first visit to Silver the houses or sites of houses we had lived in at some time she asked: "Why did you move so often?" I didn't know the answer at the time but I think I have come up with several reasons. One, which I've already mentioned is that so many of the houses we lived in were miserably cold in the winter and we always sought, sometimes without success, to better ourselves in this respect. Another reason was that as people moved away from the town more and more houses became available, and still another was that it was not much trouble for us to move because we owned so few possessions. We had no furniture and only the minimum amount of household equipment and clothes. We were poor, but not unusually poor for this town. It was a fact of life then that people were not the heavy consumers of goods that they are today, and since the goods for sale in our town were extremely limited, we were inclined not to covet what the neighbors might be able to buy. One sign of the great change that has taken place in the buying habits of people today is that many become so overloaded with possessions that they have to slough them off every so often in the form of garage sales, yard sales, and auctions. We had no such problems; we used things until they fell apart and even then did not necessarily replace them, but made do with something else.

The next move we made was our last. We lived for the next six years in a tiny four room house across the creek from the main part of town, a house that was easily heated with its kitchen range and Round Oak heater. It was quite a new house, dating from the late 1890's. It had a convenient little cellar off the kitchen which was timbered like a mine tunnel and covered with dirt on the outside. A long woodshed provided cover for the trip to our outhouse which was at the end of it. This was an especially fortunate feature of the house: many people had to go out in the elements to reach theirs.

Photo by Sadie Stoddard
Picking wild flowers in Sunday dresses.

Photo by Sadie Stoddard
The rocks were our playrounds.

Chris Conway, 1919

There were two fenced yards, one at the side of the house which had been built up with rocks to make it level and one in front which sloped down the hill. Cottonwood trees, lilac bushes and grass distinguished this house from many others in town. Most people did not bother with yards and some had no place to have one. Some fenced in big boulders and juniper trees and were quite content with that. The furniture in this house was of a much later period than the one we had moved from, but it was cheap and rickety and obviously left behind because it was not worth moving. The small dining room off the kitchen had to double as a bedroom for Sister and me. Daddy built a folding bed for us in it which was probably inspired by the one in the Heidelberger house, but it had no fancy cabinet to hide in — only a cloth curtain hid it from view. At night when we let it down it rested on "powder boxes" — the handy wooden boxes that dynamite came in for the mines. These boxes served as supplementary furniture in many miners' homes.

When I look back on our life in this snug little house I am inclined to think of it as a very happy time. But I know very well that there were hard times, unhappy times as well, and even some serious crises. For five of those years we were still children and, although we were aware of the struggle that went on to keep food on the table and pay the rent, we had enough distractions in our daily life to keep these thoughts in the background. However, when we fell on the granite rocks and tore a hole in our long black stockings, we knew that the real tragedy was not the red eye of our flesh peeking out of the hole, but the torn stocking.

One of those distractions was immediately behind the house — Morning Star Peak with its huge white dump from the mine which had made this country famous in the 1860's. The variety of rocks on this peak and a long ridge in the direction of War Eagle Mountain provided a natural playground for us. Some of the boulders were fancifully shaped suggesting chairs, beds, ships, fortresses. We made use of them for all kinds of make-believe. And we got plenty of healthful exercise climbing to the top of the peak or the ridge to look down in triumph on the crooked streets of our town and its miniaturized buildings. There is a large slanting expanse of granite exposed on the ridge and in the course of assessing its potential for play we decided that it would make an excellent slide if we had some kind of metal to

Courtesy of University Press of Idaho, Moscow, Idaho

The little house behind the schoolhouse.

The same house today.

sit on to protect our skin. On the way home we decided that the correctly shaped vessel for our fun would be Daddy's gold pan. But when we approached him on the subject he let out a cry of pain that must have been heard across town. We should have known that his gold pan was sacred. Mamma found an old wash pan with a hole in it and we had many joyous rides down that slab of granite until the pan gave out.

As we grew older we went further from home to investigate other attractions. Mamma gave us quite a bit of freedom on the condition that we go only as far as pre-arranged landmarks. If we were going "down the road" which meant down the creek, we could go as far as the first powder house which was a quarter of a mile from town, the second powder house, one half mile, or the poor house, a full mile. The powder houses were little stone buildings with corrugated iron roofs where dynamite for the mines was stored. The poor house, a square building with a flagpole, was no longer in use; the County's poor were cared for in town. If we went up the road there were three landmarks we could be timed by in this direction also. We could go to the first ice-pond which was barely out of town, the second ice-pond which was about a quarter of a mile away, or the Poorman Mill which was a full mile. Ice was still cut from these ponds in winter and stored in a sawdust filled building behind the Idaho Hotel. In summer we sometimes caught trout in the ponds with primitive equipment — a pole cut from the willows along the bank, a piece of line, and a fish hook. I once caught a good-sized trout at the second ice pond with this makeshift tackle. The Poorman Mill, which had belonged to one of the richest mines on War Eagle Mountain, still had all its machinery intact and we sometimes made use of a wide leather belt between two wheels as a slide.

Another attraction of both of these routes was the number of wild flowers along the way. We soon became expert at locating them according to the season of the year, bringing home drooping bouquets of the beauties season after season.

We settled into a routine in this little house which began with Daddy making a fire in the kitchen range in the morning. The stove was located just behind the partition of our bedroom-dining room. We were jolted awake by the load of wood he dropped into the wood box on his return trip from the woodshed and the clatter of each stove

lid as he raised it and let it fall on the stove. Making noise was one of
the joys of his life. He always laid the fire with great care and a few
muttered oaths if the ashes needed removing, and then as the fire
caught and began to roar up the stovepipe, he broke into song. He
had a large repertoire from the minstrel shows and operettas he had
heard in his youth in Kansas City, Missouri. He alternated these
with Stephen Foster ballads (he sang "Old Black Joe" with such
feeling that it brought tears to our eyes) and some Irish songs in
Gaelic which he had learned as a boy. He was so unpredictable in his
choice of songs that once he had awakened us, we couldn't possibly go
to sleep again out of curiosity about what was coming next. Smetimes
he became so joyful at the kindling of the fire that he danced up and
down the room, jigging Irish fashion, and rattling the dishes in the
cupboard. Occasionally he forgot to turn the damper in the stovepipe
and he would be too absorbed in his morning rites to notice that the
kitchen was filling up with smoke. When he finally noticed it he'd
break off in mid-song with a string of curses and soon we would hear
Mamma's despairing voice as she came in to fix breakfast.

I sometimes wonder if his joy at the kindling of the fire went back
to his ancestors in the British Isles who built bon fires and danced
around them to coax the sun back to the north. It had all the characteristics of an established rite. My sister and I had our rites, too, rites
that turned into rituals with the change of seasons. We felt a compul-
sion, for instance, to find the first buttercups in their mossy beds under the very edge of the melting snow cover, to look for the flowering
of a bed of blue camus down the road, to seek out the modest little
fritillary (we called them crocuses) under the shade of a sage or rabbit brush, to find the mid-summer columbine, forget-me-nots and
bachelor buttons up the road to the Poorman Mill. And finally in the
fall we gathered everlasting flowers whose vibrant yellow had turned
to gold with a little red heart in the center, and we cut branches off the
quaking asp whose orange-yellow leaves stood out against the dark
firs. With these souvenirs of the sun we prepared for the long dark
days of winter.

CHAPTER IV

SPRING MEMORIES

One morning our two dogs who slept in the woodshed added their voices to the tumult in the kitchen as Daddy performed his ceremonial fire-building. They did not rush into the kitchen as they usually did when he opened the door to the woodshed, and the good-natured curses he flung at them seemed to have no effect on them. Sister and I were not supposed to get up until Daddy had had his breakfast and left for the mine. But we realized that the dogs' excited state promised something unusual. We came out into the kitchen as he was opening the door to the woodshed to shout once more at the dogs. To our surprise a long white furry creature dashed into the kitchen, paused a moment in confusion, and then streaked through our bedroom-dining-room to a window where Mamma kept some potted plants. Daddy had slammed the door to the woodshed before the dogs could get in and they were now throwing themselves against it and barking hysterically. When our white furry visitor saw that the window was not a way to freedom, he turned a frantic face toward us and Daddy leaped to his rescue just as the latch to the woodshed door gave way and the dogs burst in, following the trail of their quarry with agonized yelps. He closed the window inches from their noses as the weasel in its white winter coat leaped to freedom and blended with the snow.

We were so happy about the event and its outcome that we didn't notice that Mamma had come into the kitchen until she let out an agonized cry. When we saw her with her hands covering her nose, we, too, became aware of what our excitement had prevented us from noticing: our charming white-coated visitor had left a trail of odor as strong as a skunk's.

Still holding her nose with one hand Mamma opened doors and windows and brought out the scrub bucket and mop. Unfortunately her efforts with soap and water seemed to make matters worse. The odor penetrated the nose like pure amonia, and it hung around our breakfast table with such persistence that only Daddy, in a manic state of good humor because of his rescue of the weasel, could eat a bite. Mamma told us to put on our winter coats and take our toast and cocoa out on the steps of the front porch.

The excitement of the wild creature's visit and the novelty of eating breakfast in the open air have fixed the memory of that bright morning in my mind so that whenever I hear the word "spring" I can see and hear it all again. It wasn't spring yet, as all the snow around us testified, but the promise of spring was in every sight and sound. A warm wind striking the snow banks made them tick like clocks and the giant icicles from our roof had stabbed them deeply. The sun just peaking over War Eagle Mountain lit up the bare cottonwood trees whose iced twigs pock marked the snow under them with every iridescent drop. And underneath the shrinking snow, the creeks were raging to break through. As we sat sipping our cocoa in the bright sunshine we were happy not only for the weasel's return to the wilds, but for the promise of freedom spring held out to us — freedom from school, from dark winter days, and from the heavy, confining, clothes we had to wear.

On another spring morning we set out on an excursion that was even more of a departure from our routine. Members of our church in Silver had made arrangements with a priest and his parish in Jordan Valley, Oregon, to meet at the only Catholic cemetery in the region for a Mass on "Decoration Day," as we called Memorial Day then. Friends had invited us to go with them in their car — a lucky break for us, for we had no means of transportation. The prospect of riding in a car was, in itself, unusual enough for us to make this outing exciting. In addition a picnic was planned after Mass, and we looked forward to the the novelty of a church service held out of doors.

We usually heard Mass in a big white frame building across the street from the hotel. Our Lady of Tears Church had once been a boarding house which had been remodeled in a rather slip-shod manner. To give an air of spaciousness to the main section of the church, the second story floor had been removed. It had been retained in the rear section to make a choir loft. Under the choir loft was a hall with a narrow stairway and two small rooms — a confessional and a tiny bedroom for the visiting priest. The narrow stairs and the floor of the loft were very shaky. The boards creaked under our feet when we were sent upstairs to pull the rope which rang the bell for mass. The fragile nature of this part of the building and the impossibility of heating it in the winter tended to shorten confessions, and the priests abjured the tiny bedroom in favor of the hotel across the street.

An arrangement of church-like windows and a coat of white paint on its front side gave the church a respectable appearance when seen from the hotel porch, but, like many mining town buildings, its south side where a neighboring building had been torn down, was innocent of paint. By the 1920s the building had begun to lean for support against the north-side neighbor. Its overall sad appearance convinced me that this must have been the reason for calling it "Our Lady of Tears."

Services were scheduled here even in winter months when the priest had to come in on the sleigh that brought the mail. But attendance declined a lot in winter when the weather was bad. One couple who didn't let the weather or the cold church stand in their way lived in a spot that would have been a perfect excuse for non-attendance with less devout people. Aunt Annie and Uncle Mockie Dugan lived at the Blaine mine up Long Gulch, a steep climb from Silver and a gulch well known for avalanches. They had come to the Blaine when Aunt Annie's nephew, Pete Steele, opened up the old tunnel to look for ore that had been missed in earlier times. Uncle Mockie worked in the mine and Aunt Annie helped Pete's wife with the household chores. They were from Scranton, Pennsylvania, where Uncle Mockie had worked in the coal mines.

On summer Sundays when we were not having mass at Our Lady of Tears, Aunt Annie came down the gulch to say the rosary with us in the church and to hear our catechism. Sister and I used to walk up the gulch to meet her, picking flowers along the way to put on the altar. I can still see her as she appeared on the trail ahead of us, small and frail in clothes that dated from the 1890s — a long blue serge skirt, a white blouse with leg-o'mutton sleeves, and a navy blue straw "sailor" hat. She carried a stout stick as a staff in one hand and her prayerbook in the other. Her face, red from the heat, creased in smiles when she saw us and she always cried out: "Isn't it grand?" When we drew her attention to our wild bouquets she would say:

"Aren't they grand?" Things that were "grand" were so wonderful to her that they made her eyes tear with happiness. We considered her every bit the equal of the saints of the Church we had read about.

Uncle Mockie was almost as much of a saint as she was. The worst that could be said of him was that he didn't mind a few drinks with the "boys" occasionally. He dressed for church in a modest costume of flannel shirt and pants held up by suspenders. He had a pair of shoes that he polished to perfection for the occasion, shoes which had big round toes like half a baseball. He always stood with his head on one side as if he were asking for mercy and it seemed to me that the toes of his shoes were looking up at him.

When it was our turn to provide a meal for the priest while he was in town we always included Aunt Annie and Uncle Mockie in the invitation. I think Mamma was slightly nervous about having the priest in our house because of my father's agnostic beliefs, and Uncle Mockie, who was extremely garrulous on the subject of the Pennsylvania mines, could be counted on to distract Daddy so that he would not demand of the priest if he knew that the earth was several billion years old. Often times when Sister and I were memorizing our catechism by asking questions of each other, he would interrupt us on the subject of the Creation to give us his version according to Lyell and Darwin.

The prospect of the trip away from home, though it was only twenty miles, the novelty of the outdoor mass, and the proposed picnic, kept us in a state of excitement for days. Someone in town, perhaps motivated by jealousy, threw a slight chill on our anticipation by telling us that the grove we planned to picnic in was a haven for rattlesnakes. We did not have them in Silver because of our high altitude so we knew them only by their dreadful reputation. Our informant made matters worse by telling about a picnic where a snake took the opportunity offered by an unguarded lunch under the trees to make off with a hard boiled egg. Mamma was so upset by the tale that she told us we were not to leave her side during the whole affair.

We were happy when we awoke on the morning of the excursion to see that the day was sunny and mild, and not, as sometimes happened this time of year, darkened by clouds which might suddenly envelop us in snow or sleet. We still had patches of snow on the mountains around us and icy rivulets ran over rocks which in another month would be bone dry. The road was muddy in spots as the car we rode in edged down the creek, dropping into warmer air as we went. The canyon where the deserted town of Delamar lay was already dusty. We waved to our friend, the watchman of the mine, who stood on the porch of the hotel watching our caravan with curious eyes. Three miles more brought us to the pile of tailings which marked the site of the vanished town of Wagontown. Beyond it we came to the cottonwood grove.

The parishioners from Jordan Valley had arrived before us and had already spread their blankets under the trees. Many of them were Basques who had come to this country from Spain, first as sheepherders and later as owners of the huge flocks they pastured in the valleys in winter and in our mountains in summer. Many of them had relatives who were buried in the cemetery which was just over a ridge from the grove. The priest had not yet arrived. He would be with us, we were told, shortly after he had said his last mass of the day at his parish.

We stripped off the heavy sweaters we had put on in the chill of the morning at home. The air was suffocatingly hot even at this early hour. Not a hint of breeze stirred the old cottonwoods and we soon found that their shade was very unlike the cool shadows cast by trees in the mountains.

We spread our blankets after a careful look around and sat down warily, although our fellow picnickers assured us that they had scouted the area for snakes and found none. Aunt Annie settled down with us while Uncle Mockie went off to fraternize with the men. Mamma reminded us that we were confined to the limits of the blankets and we resigned ourselves to the boredom of waiting. We watched the road in the direction the priest's car would come and were occasionally fooled by a dust-devil which mimicked the dust trail of a car. We had not eaten breakfast that morning because we planned to receive communion at Mass. (In those days you did not eat after midnight if you were to receive communion in the morning.) Unaccustomed to the stifling heat and painfully aware of our empty stomachs, gritty with dust from the open car, we kept our boring vigil while the crowd around us hummed an unintelligible mixture of Basque and English. The shade of the cottonwoods shrank as the sun approached the zenith. Hours were passing and nothing at all was happening on this day we had looked forward to for so long. Even Aunt Annie, her face bright red under her hat, couldn't find anything to call "grand."

As the hours slipped away some of the picnickers gave up fasting. Voices around us became more animated as the Basques brought out their wine-skins and other men opened bottles. Mamma worried about our empty stomachs and tried to tempt us with food, but we had resolved to participate in this outing to the full, communion and all, and we were not ready to give up yet. After Mamma wiped my gritty face with her handkerchief I took her suggestion and put my head down in her lap and closed my eyes.

I was dozing when Aunt Annie's voice, loud with anguish, jolted me awake. "Mockie! Mockie!" She cried. In my half awake state I could think of only one thing — rattlesnakes. I jumped up and looked around the blanket and out into the sage brush around us, believing so strongly in my delusion that I thought I could see them advancing on us. Mamma was pulling on my skirt to make me sit down. The crowd was suddenly quiet. Aunt Annie had left our blanket and was standing at the edge of the crowd of men. Among them I saw Uncle Mockie's tilted face and, as he talked to Aunt Annie, he was gesturing with a bottle he held in his hand. I knew then what had caused Aunt Annie's agonized cry. Uncle Mockie had got carried away by the fellowship of the crowd and tipped up the bottle as it was passed. Aunt Annie had seen him and tried to stop him before he broke his fast. We knew she had been too late when she came back to our blanket with her sailor hat awry and tears staining her cheeks.

The fact that Uncle Mockie would not be able to receive communion was a real tragedy for her, because we lived in a place where Mass was heard infrequently and the opportunity to be in a state of grace again might be months away. Her sadness as she wiped away her tears deepened the misery of our long wait. We had almost given up the idea of the outdoor mass when we heard the sound of a motor and saw a car churning up the alkali dust of the desert road. The priest was wearing brown coveralls, well-dusted by the trip, and his face and those of the boys with him who were to serve mass were streaked with sweat and dust. They had had the misfortunes of having to change a tire in the bare, hot, desert country.

The boys opened the suitcases which contained the vestments

and props for mass and the priest slipped the stole around his neck
and announced that confessions would be heard on the other side of
his car. Many in the crowd had succumbed to the temptation of food
or drink, so there was not a long delay before the boys began helping
the priest into his white surplice and the black vestments for the mass
for the dead. The boys walked ahead up the hill with the cross and
the book, and the priest followed with the chalice under its black
cloth. We followed along the dim trail through the sage brush, up
over the ridge, and into the deserted cemetery.

Like other ghost town cemeteries, this one was uncared for. Sage
brush and wild flowers had taken over, and the stones were hidden in
the thick growth. Someone had set up a table for an altar and cleared
a place of brush large enough for the crowd to kneel in. The ritual of
Mass proceeded according to the old style, with prayers and re-
sponses in Latin.

The picnic after the service fulfilled some of my expectations of
the day, but Aunt Annie's bitter disappointment, the heat, and the
long delay left me with mixed feelings about this long-awaited spring
excursion.

Photo Courtesy of Robert T. Blake
From left: Chris Conway, Charlie Blake, Mockie Dugan, Josephine Conway, Elizabeth Conway, Annie
Dugan. Children: Robert Blake, Charles Blake, Julia Conway.

CHAPTER V

THE RITES OF SUMMER

After the end of World War I the mines in the Owyhees operated by fits and starts. Steady work at a big paying mine was a thing of the past. And sometimes crews were hired by speculators who didn't have the money to meet even one payroll. The men and their families suffered from lost wages, and, even if they were paid, the wages were lower than the ones they'd been used to during the War. Why did we and others continue to live in a place where the market for labor was so poor? We were sustained by a dream not unlike the dreams that brought people to this part of the country in the first place — a dream of finding lost veins of rich ore, especially veins on War Eagle Mountain whose many faults and fractures had dramatically cut off the rich ore of the 1860's. The dreams were embodied for nearly every family in town by the claims they owned, but the very ownership of them made us poorer still for in order to keep them a man had to do one hundred dollars worth of work on them every year. That meant an employed miner had to quit a paying job to do the work or hire someone else to do it. If he moved away the chances were that he would barely be able to meet expenses: saving up money to have the work done on several claims was not easy in the 1920's. So some of us stayed on, living on short rations and high hopes.

Like most children we didn't worry a lot about the financial situation at home, and the fact that our mother did and our father didn't made us prefer his cheerful company. One of the summer excursions with him that we looked forward to was his first trip of the year to his claims on War Eagle to take up supplies to do his assessment work. All the work he did on them was done by hand in the very way claims were worked in the early days. He drilled the holes at the face of his tunnels by driving steel drills into the rock with a "double-jack", a large hammer resembling a wood-splitting maul. He loaded the holes with dynamite, attached fuses and caps, and blew out the rock. He carried the muck out by wheelbarrow. The only real difference between him and a miner of the 1860's was that he had modern dynamite rather than black powder, and improved fuses and caps.

The first trip we made with him, when I was seven and Sister was nine, initiated a ritual that we insisted on as one of our rights. But we came close on that first occasion to disgracing ourselves as mountain climbers and I was to bear the stigma of having acted like a baby for many years. We started out in the cool of the morning up the road past the ice ponds. Daddy had a pack of tools — the steel drills, the double-jack, and the explosives — on his back and we carried two tin lard buckets with our lunch. He walked slowly and steadily while we ran ahead, making side trips up the rock slopes on our right and down to the creek on our left. A few times he said to us with more amusement than reproof: "You kids are going to be dead tired before we even start up the mountain." We couldn't imagine being tired in the course of this glorious expedition, so we went on running, climbing, exploring anything that caught our eye.

When we left the road to follow the trail up the mountain the mid-morning sun beat down on us. The rocks which had been a delightful challenge along the road became a sudden enemy as our feet slid on them and we scraped our knees as we slid. We had to tie our lard buckets to our belts so we could grasp shrubs and even weeds to pull ourselves along. A few steps left us breathless as the icy mountain air filled our lungs. We could barely keep Daddy in sight now as he moved at the same steady pace he had kept to on the road.

When we stopped to catch our breath we could look back and see our town far below us looking like a play-town with its flat roofs and crooked streets. We had looked down on it before from Morning Star Peak but now we were far above it and it looked much tinier because we could see the great mountains that surrounded it on all sides. We stumbled on after these pauses panting and gasping and pulling desperately at anything we could catch hold of with our thorn-pierced fingers.

With every stop we made Daddy gained on us and it was hard to keep him in sight as he walked on at the same steady pace. When he paused once to look back at us I conceived a desperate plan and started toward him as fast as I could go, with my lard bucket banging painfully against me. I yelled "Wait!" as loud as I could in my breathless state and when I caught up with him I held on to his coat so he wouldn't start on again. He waited patiently until I had recovered enough breath to talk. "Daddy," I said. "Could you carry me the rest of the way?" He let out one of his earsplitting howls followed by peals of laughter. "Carry you?" he shouted. "A big girl like you?" (I was really rather small for my age.) And as Sister came stumbling up he began one of his kindly, reasonable, sermonettes. "Now, kids," he began. "I know how you love to run and play and, if you recall, I told you on the way up the road that you were going to be worn out when we started the climb. Sister, you and Dude, here (Dude was my Silver City nickname), are getting to be big girls now, and if you're going to go up to the claims with me, you're going to have to learn to climb. So . . ." He left the lesson for us to complete, turned his back on us, and went on up the mountain. We followed, close to tears as we fell, scraping off more skin, sweating from the hot sun, chilled a minute later by an icy breeze. At last we saw him on a mine dump above us signaling that this was our destination. When we reached it we threw ourselves down, too tired to walk to the mouth of the tunnel to get a drink.

Daddy was whistling cheerfully as he gathered dry pieces off the tops of sage brush for a fire. He took a piece of paper out of his pack sack and arranged the fire with his usual precision. When he was ready to light it he began patting his pockets and looking at us in a pained way to show us that something was wrong. "If I didn't go and forget matches!" he shouted. This was the worst news we could have heard at the moment for Mamma had put wieners in our lunch buckets as a special treat with the warning that they must be boiled thoroughly before we ate them. She believed that eating raw wieners led inevitably to becoming a host to tape-worm. The tears we had been fighting for some time began in earnest now as we faced this terrible disappointment. Daddy was keeping an eye on us and I think now that his ruse of "no matches" was designed to bring us out of the bad mood we'd fallen into.

"Oh, well," he said cheerfully. "We'll make a fire without matches." He turned to the carefully laid fire and we jumped up to see the promised miracle. He took out his quartz glass and held it over the paper so that the sun shone through the lenses. A hole with brown edges appeared in the paper, curls of sage-drenched smoke rose up, and the fire crackled. Wonder and delight replaced our mood of misery and we ran to fill a pail from the water at the mouth of the tunnel.

We made this trip with him year after year and we learned after this first one to restrain ourselves as we walked along the road, to save our energy for the steep climb. The lesson was especially sharp for me because I had to hear many times how I, a seven year old girl, had begged to be carried.

Sometimes in later years after we'd had our lunch we'd climb still further up the mountain to see Daddy's best friend and fellow prospector — Andy Swan. We were as fond of this man as Daddy was, for he always remembered our names and didn't confuse us as many people did because both our names started with the letter J. He didn't call me Dude, but said my real name with such a charming lilt that I wished everyone would call me that. "Josephine and Julia," he'd say softly in the slight Canadian accent that made his speech unique. "And how is your mother?" He was a thin, agile, man with a gentle voice — a great contrast to my father. But these two, such different types, shared a consuming passion — the pursuit of those elusive veins of ore on War Eagle Mountain. After Andy had paid his polite respects to us he took Daddy over to the latest pile of ore he'd got out and they examined it together, picking up piece after piece and anlyzing it, and sometimes pounding up some of it in a little hand mortar and panning it out to see what "colors" they got. Sometimes they squatted for hours on that mine dump, drawing impromptu maps on its surface to represent the way they thought the lodes ran on that mountain. We played in the shade and half-listened to their contented voices.

Another summer outing we enjoyed with my father was woodgathering. His favorite method was to blow out the big stumps left when the virgin timber was cut in the early days, for he loved any activity that involved the use of "powder." But as the stumps became scarcer he sometimes had to pit his strength against that odd plant which grows in some mountain-desert locations — mountain mahogany. He had developed mighty arm and wrist muscles from swinging a double-jack in the mines and, since he was already of athletic build from a youthful career as a boxer, it was not as difficult for him to chop out a clump of the scraggly shrub as it would have been for a novice. The hardness and weight of this plant make it an excellent fuel. It is so heavy that it will not float in water and it burns slow-ly, leaving little ash. Pioneers recognized its value as a fuel, and even when I lived in Silver wood-cutters still pulled loads of the twisted grayish canes, so gnarled they were almost impossible to stack, into town. It is not related to the mahogany tree of tropical countries, but its fine-grained wood takes an excellent polish, and if you can find a straight cane among the twisted limbs, you can make an attractive walking stick. My father made these in his spare time as presents for my mother's brothers. Since they were better off than she was, she could in this way give them a present that cost nothing but was nevertheless a present. After he had peeled and polished the canes he burned patterns on them with his carbide lamp. They were very at-tractive. I know of only one that has survived.

I have an affection for this plant that can't really be justified by its appearance. Its grayish bark and tiny leathery leaves can't be called things of beauty. But my associations with it have endeared it to me for other reasons. When the brittle little leaves pile up around the base of the clump they make a crisp, fragrant bed to rest on. And when you sift them through your fingers they give off a pleasant spicy aroma. They have another attraction: after their insignificant blossoms die off, seeds like fine curled feathers cover them. A moun-tain side glowing in the sun with the golden feathered shrubs is an-other delight.

When we were lucky enough to find stumps for dynamiting Sis-ter and I often rested in the shade, or rather semi-shade, of a ma-hogany clump, enjoying its fragrance as we sifted the dried leaves through our fingers, while we waited for Daddy to bore holes at the base of the stump and load them with sticks of powder. When he had the fuses ready to light he'd find a big boulder some distance away for us to shelter behind. When he'd lit them he'd come running and we'd huddle together with our hands over our eyes. Sometimes little rocks and sticks peppered us after the explosion. When we had collected the pieces of wood and dragged them down to the road where a man with a team would pick them up, we got out our lunch as Daddy shouted in his usual exuberant way: "Give me a drink of that tea! I'm drier then a wooden god!"

Mahogony in bloom.

CHAPTER VI

HOME MADE PLEASURES

These excursions with my father were the exception as far as entertainment went. On most summer days we had to fall back on our own resources for amusement. Paper dolls cut from mail-order catalogues helped pass the time while we waited for the stage to rumble over the bridge, a signal for our daily pilgrimage to the Post Office. Every summer the post-mistress cleaned out the stacks of catalogues sent to people who had long since left town and piled them behind her living quarters in the Post Office. Then when we and other children came for the mail she invited us to go out in back and help ourselves. The pile looked to us like pure gold and we happily crawled around on its slippery surface looking for another odd piece for our collection. Some we saved for winter cutting but many were so tempting that we sat down immediately on our front porch cutting with wild abandon and anchoring each cut-out with a rock so it wouldn't blow away.

But our catalogues paled in comparison to another treasure which our friend Emma brought one day — movie magazines. They were the first we had ever seen. We hadn't seen more than a half-dozen movies in our lives on our visits to Boise. We became instant fans and, after we had leafed through the books, the names of Mae Murray, Anita Stewart, Betty Compson, the Gish Sisters, Ethel Clayton, the Talmedge Sisters, and Mary Pickford became as familiar to us as the names of people in Silver. We were surprised when Mamma rejected the pictures we had cut out as wall decorations.

At about the same time we fell heir to another gift so rich and dazzling that it taxed our inventiveness beyond its limits — the jewel encrusted crowns, the robes and capes of a defunct lodge. It was fun to dress up in them and parade around at first, but we soon tired of admiring each other and the robes joined the rejected movie queens in a box.

One day when we were exploring the hillside behind us we

pushed open the door of a little shed behind an empty house. The tiny building with its one small window looked like a perfect secret hideaway. I don't know which of us — Sister, our friend Emma or I — thought up the scheme we carried out. The little isolated shed, the pictures of our idols, and the elegant robes, suddenly evolved into a type of play that had all the elements children of our ages love: secrecy, privacy from prying eyes, ritual, and idol worship. We spirited the box of our treasures out of the house, decorated the walls with the pictures of the movie queens, giving the place of honor to a young woman, Olive Thomas, who had been featured in color on the cover of *PhotoPlay* because she had killed herself. The ritual we finally adopted was a compromise. The only ones Sister and I knew were those of the Catholic Church. Emma was not a Catholic but she was knowledgeable about the ceremonies of certain lodges. I don't remember now the details we worked out together, except that Sister and I held out for genuflecting in front of Olive Thomas. The robes and crowns played their part as either the vestments of an imitation Mass or the robes of lodge ceremonies. We called the little shed "The Mystic Shrine" — a name furnished by Emma.

Children love secrets but are naive about keeping them. Mamma's curiosity was aroused by our whispering and conspiratorial air. One day she asked what had happened to our box of fancy robes. We said it was outside but we would bring it in immediately. We scampered off to our hideout and brought it back, believing that our secret was still inviolate. But Mamma must have made it a point to see where we went. She had no doubt been curious about our daily unannounced disappearances. With the ceremonial robes at home we thought we had allayed her suspicions and the next day, resigned to carrying out our rituals in a defrocked state, we visited the Mystic Shrine for the last time. We were shocked to find when we arrived at the little shed, that someone had nailed and boarded up the window and door. We were stunned, not only at the loss of our hide-away, but also because our secret was known. When we got up our courage to peek through the cracks of the door, we saw our forsaken movie idols staring at each other on the walls.

Gathering wild flowers was the entertainment of last resort when everything else had failed us. The few pictures I have from our childhood often show us with bouquets. We became quite knowledgeable about where to find each kind in its proper season. We knew where wild camus grew in profusion near the Knights of Pythias cemetery, where wild iris flourished in a marshy spot on War Eagle Mountain. We were captivated by the sight of dainty bitter root on the bare summits, but these and stonecrop we couldn't add to our bouquets because they had no stems to hold on to. Everything else we plucked ruthlessly. We even tried to break the tough stems of mountain penstemon, whose lovely purple bells made spots of color in the gray rocks. Forget-me-nots, bachelor's buttons, Indian paintbrush, white and yellow balsam, columbine, bluebells, wild roses, and many others grew along the road to the iceponds. There were rarer plants more precious for having to be searched for — modest little fritillaries hid under sage brush, delicate lavendar steer heads with their intriguing horns, and tiny orchids or ladyslippers were rare enough to be considered prizes. The more delicate ones arrived at home in a state of irreversible wilt, but the triumph of finding them made them worth the effort.

In the course of these expeditions we took time to explore cemeteries and read the names on tombstones. Many of the names were already familiar to us as the names of townspeople. Others we had heard about when people talked about the early days. We even had our favorites among the gravestones and sometimes left each a wild bouquet. I always think of my favorite one as the "bride stone" although I know very well that the marker is really a vase with a marble drapery flowing around it, set on a pedestal. It is one of the largest stones in the cemetery on Florida Mountain and is clearly visible from town from which point it looks like a bride dressed in white with a veil. Even though I knew the name of the man this stone commemorated and saw his wife and daughters nearly every day I still thought of it as the "bride stone."

We often came home from these expeditions resembling our bouquets — drooping and wilted from the summer sun. We usually carried water or lemonade with us in handy little bottles with glass stoppers and rubber washers which came to our house filled with Daddy's favorite physic — citrate of magnesia — whose effectiveness he often testified to, with fervent oaths. It didn't matter if we dropped one on the rocks and broke it for we knew he'd soon be getting another one at the drugstore.

CHAPTER VII

THE HAUNTED HOUSE

The Owyhee Mountains are at their best in the fall. Perhaps Florida Mountain in Silver was named in this season, for the turning of the aspens, choke cherries, and a myriad of small colorful shrubs against the background of its rocks and firs justifies such a flowery name. After the first hard freeze of the year we used to go up an old mine road on it to pick choke cherries. Mamma made a bitter-sweet jelly out of them. The frost made them sweeter, but they still puckered our mouths as we ate and picked. We could have cut our aspen branches here, too, but we didn't because we had a special place for that — a spot up the creek on the side of a hill in a thick growth of the misshapen little trees.

There was an old house in the grove whose doors and windows had been removed for use elsewhere. The dark windowless holes staring out of the brilliant trees made a deep impression on us and we decided to call this "The Haunted House." We probably wouldn't have thought of it if we had not been under the influence of a series of girl-heroine books involving such romantic adventures as trips to haunted houses.

We didn't share the name or the spot with any of our friends for fear, I think, of being laughed at. We had already had that experience with other flights of our fancy. But one time when we were playing with other children we let slip a reference to it. "What haunted house?" They wanted to know. We tried at first to evade the question but that only made them more curious. We ended by pointing out the house in the grove. That didn't satisfy our questioners. They wanted to know on what authority its hauntedness rested. If we had been bold enough to make up a ghost tale we could have made a decent case for ourselves. Instead we confessed that we had given it the name because it *looked* haunted. What we had meant to avoid by keeping it a secret happened now with a vengeance; we were not only laughed at, we were accused of "making up things" — the next step from telling lies.

I hadn't thought about the place and its associations for a long time until, on a recent trip to Silver, we picnicked at a spot along the creek under the hill with the aspen grove. The old house was gone, but after lunch I decided to walk up the hill and see if I could find any trace of it. The climb was much steeper than I remembered and I stumbled around among the roots of the trees for a long time before I found it. A few of its foundation stones and a pile of broken chimney bricks showed me where it had been. Some of the bricks on the bottom of the pile had turned to dust and left a red stain on the ground.

I had a greater sense of loss about this old house than I had had about the many other vanished places I had known in Silver. Even houses we had once lived in didn't seem as important as this one. I stood there in the golden light of the little trees trying to figure out

The "haunted house" stood in this grove of aspen.

why this place affected me more than the others. Why had I taken the pains to climb up here in my old age to look for something I knew wasn't there?

The sharp October wind struck the grove as I stood wondering about it. The leaves broke into their delicate applause and the bright light, shattered by their constant turning, fell around me like rain. That sound, that light, thrilled me as it had in my childhood. The old house, even though there was nothing left of it but the stained earth and a few stones, meant more to me because it was something we had created. Coming here to pick the boughs we had had an experience with the beauty of the place and by naming it "The Haunted House" we had made it a part of ourselves.

CHAPTER VIII

WINTER: OUTDOOR FUN AND INDOOR VISITS

Although winter was long and confining we enjoyed it because it provided the essentials for the traditional sports of the town — skiing and bob-sledding. Some winters the snow was very heavy and skis and snowshoes were the only way of getting around. I can remember seeing my father set off for his job at a mine on his skis with his snowshoes on his back. When he left town he changed to the snowshoes for the climb up the mountain. On the way home he skied all the way. My mother used to stand at the front window when he worked at a mine up Long Gulch waiting for him and the other men to appear at a certain spot which could be seen from our house. We knew when we saw her there that she was worrying about the avalanches the gulch was famous for. When at last the men came sliding down they looked like pieces of soot drifting down a white page. She would sigh with relief then and hurry out to the kitchen to finish preparing supper.

We learned to ski just as city children learn to roller skate — by trial and error. Our skis were locally made by several men. Some took the pains to paint them beautifully, but others just gave them a plain coat. The second pair of skis I owned was given to me by a boy who was moving out to the valley. They were painted with an intricate design in gray, black, and white. I could scarcely believe my good fortune when I inherited them. They were nothing like modern skis. All that kept them on your feet was a piece of leather and a wooden cleat to keep your foot from sliding forward. We carried a single rather long pole to anchor ourselves as we climbed hills and to balance ourselves on the way down. The worst feature of the skis was that if you fell, one or both could escape and go bobbing off down the hill before you could pick yourself up. The first time I tried to ski on Florida Mountain with the "big kids" I had this discouraging experience and

Photo Courtesy of Idaho Historical Society
Snowdrifts on the main street of town.

after chasing an errant ski downhill I was too cold to go up and try
again.

Bob-sledding called for quite a bit of effort and preparation. The
blacksmith made the small sleds which were bolted to a large plank.
The boy (more often a young man) who sat in front had the responsi-
bility for guiding it and advising the riders when to lean on curves.
There were spills, of course, but no one that I knew was injured seriously. We didn't lack some good exciting slopes and the track took
advantage of the best which was through the middle of town, starting
on Potosi Peak, turning on the upper end of the street the Courthouse
was on, turning again on the short street which was once called "Avalanche," and again on the street in front of the Idaho Hotel where it
plunged down the hill which leads into town, across the bridge, and
as far up the next rise as momentum would carry us. Young men and
boys iced the track with buckets of water on very cold nights for some
time before it was considered fit for use. When at last it was ready the

sled roared through town under the billiant stars or the moon with its passengers screaming with delight and terror.

I realize now that winter wasn't fun for everyone. For people like my mother who didn't have suitable clothes to go out in except on well broken trails, it must have been very confining. But she did go out whenever she could to indulge in the only recreation open to women in those days — visiting. I can't help feeling sad that this institution has come upon hard times since the advent of television. We make a great thing of being "people oriented" now; even banks claim that their business is people. But we have moved away from being interested in real people. We are often wrapped up in television personalities or even in the roles they play.

Sister and I usually went along when Mamma went visiting, sometimes with joyful anticipation, sometimes unenthusiastically. We didn't like to turn down a chance to go with her for fear that we might miss some bit of gossip or news. The people of Silver and their doings were immensely interesting to us. Perhaps this was so because we hadn't today's distractions in the way of entertainment. But I think two other factors played a part in it: one was the town itself which, like many western towns, gloried in its "characters." The stories and jokes we passed around about each other were our entertainment. Writers like Mark Twain and Brete Harte made it their bread and butter. The other factor in our case was my father. He was interested in where people came from, how they talked, what their physical mannerism were. I can remember how delighted he was when Sister and I came home from town and reported to him that Charlie Comish, an old miner, had called our dog who was always at our heels "an *auld* red-faced thing." He repeated the phrase in a jubilant shout and then said in a tone of respect: "You know, Charlie is from the Isle of Man." He said this as if it were an honor and then he went on to instruct us that the Isle of Man was in the Irish sea between England and Ireland. After we had reported Charlie's phrase to him he often referred to Shep as "that auld red-faced thing." Another man in town, Gibb the tailor, he often told us, was from Wales, where they had huge mines, so that this old man was doubly honored: he was Welsh and he came from a mining country. It was not just people from the British Isles that he took an interest in. Chinese, Italians, Swedes, and all the other nationalities found in mining camps interested him by their uniqueness. If any one of them could be said to be his favorite I think it would have been the Italians. When the Boise paper carried the headline "The Golden Voice Is Silent," announcing the death of Caruso, his face showed real pain and he became unusually quiet.

So the talk we heard when we went visiting with Mamma did not bore us. We were already pre-disposed to enjoy the mannerisms, the odd accents, the little jokes, and the occasional exciting gossip. And when the talk turned to events of the past and of people long dead it gave us a glimpse of something else — the history of the place we lived in.

One of the women we especially liked to visit had come to the region in the very early days, not to Silver, but to a little town named Fairview, now completely gone, near the very top of War Eagle Mountain.

She came from New York City by way of San Francisco, coming once, as she put it, "around the Hown" and another time after she went back for a visit, across the hump in Panama. She probably couldn't have found a greater contrast to her native city than the little jerry-built town of Fairview perched near the summit on the windswept east side of War Eagle. The reason for its existence was the fact that the great mines of that period — the Oro Fino, the Poorman, the Golden Chariot, and the Ida Elmore — were nearby. These mines were not only fabulously rich but their richness inspired enough greed so that two of them — the Golden Chariot and the Ida Elmore — engaged in a shooting war over disputed veins, resulting in the deaths of several men, and another — the Poorman — erected a fortress on its property to stave off a threatened attack.

She was proud of the fact that she had brought the first rocking chair to this uncivilized land. (I wish I could reproduce the way she said "chair" but I don't think it's possible. I heard the same accent years later in the speeches of Franklin Roosevelt.) Unfortunately this relic was destroyed in a fire in the 1870's which leveled the town of Fairview. She moved to Silver then and her husband prospered in the hotel business.

Her stories were not about the events that were recorded as the history of this place. They were the small domestic crises in the life of a wife and mother in those times. Perhaps that is why they appealed to us so much. And then, too, she told them with much laughter and good humor, although some must have been trying experiences.

One of her stories made such an impression on me that I can still hear her telling it in her delightful accent. It happened at the end of her visit to New York when her children were small. She had secured passage on a ship to begin the long journey back to California and had made all the arrangements necessary for a mother traveling with three children. On the very day they were to board the ship, the youngest child uncooperatively broke out with measles. There was nothing a ship's captain feared more than a raging contagion on board during a trip that called for close contact with passengers and crew for months. So each passenger met with close scrutiny from the Captain's eyes as he came on board. The young mother knew that if she cancelled her passage now she would have to wait months for another ship and wouldn't see her home in the West again for more than a year. She decided to take a chance on getting by the captain. She coached little Ed, the measle-stricken child, to hide his face in the folds of her long skirt as they went on board. All went well until at the critical moment Ed was overcome with curiosity and peeked out. The Captain who had been about to wave them on caught sight of his red-blotched face and let out a cry for them to halt. "Madame!" he cried. "What's wrong with that little shaver's face?" At this point in her story she always laughed so heartily that she had to take off her glasses and wipe them. The little shaver was diagnosed as a measles victim and he and the rest of the famly spent some time in the pest house in New York Harbor while their ship sailed without them.

This pioneer lady's good nature and sense of humor made her our favorite "visitee." And, in addition, her house was full of little treasures that spoke to us about that glamorous city she came from. She liked to tell about each object in her china closet as we pointed them out to her. The treasure I admired most was an apple stuck all over with whole cloves about which she always said: "That apple is ovah a hundred yeahs old!" One hundred years seemed like a very long time to me. What we called "the early days" in this country were only sixty years in the past.

Sometimes she brought out a music box and let us listen to its tinkling tunes. Another entertainment she provided was an elaborate sterioptican in a polished wood case which she set up on chairs for us to use. There were two cylinders inside with two sets of cards so we could both look into it at the same time, turning the cylinders with knobs on the side of the box. On the top of the box there were some stained glass panels you could adjust to color the scenes. Some were photographs of famous places, some artist's conceptions of historic events. And then there were photographs which were quite puzzling to us. One of them made me so curious that I had to ask about it. A lady was undressing in the presence of a man in a derby hat. (She had got only as far as her petticoat.) Our hostess looked at it and laughed. "Oh, deah!" she gasped. "I'm afraid some of those cahds are not very nice!" The sterioptican had been in the bar-room of her husband's hotel she explained and some of the pictures were meant for the entertainment of male patrons. However, the scenes remained in the box and we continued to puzzle over them.

The front window of her house was always bright with blooms of her potted geraniums which she grew in the green and gold cans that Ed's favorite tobacco came in. I have never known anyone who had such success with geraniums and I think her secret was that she was always nipping them off with her dainty little fingers to keep them from getting "leggy." They were thick and green, and the blooms were red, salmon, pink, and white. When I walk up that street today I half-expect to see that blaze of color in the window of the old house.

Another pioneer lady we visited was a decided contrast to our favorite. At her house we sat on straight, uncomfortable chairs and stayed out of the conversation. Nothing at all was provided for our amusement; a case of the fidgets drew a stern warning look from her. There were a few copies of her son's favorite reading material on a table that we could look at out of desperation but these — "Argosy," "Blue Book," and "Western Story" — with their pulpy pages and fine print offered little distraction. The only diversion, if you could call it that, was her big, black, mean, tom-cat, whom we were forbidden to touch. He used to come parading into the living room letting out hoarse, petulant, meows, supremely confident of his mistress' reaction, which was always a startled cry: "Why, Tom! What's the matter?" If he sat down in the middle of the room and kept up his unpleasant meowing she would jump up and go to the kitchen to fix some cat-treat for him. He'd walk after her with a self satisfied air, giving a token caress to the door-jam on the way. If he went toward the front door with his urgent meows she'd jump out of her little rocker and have the door open by the time he got there. He knew that he was king of the patch.

Sometimes he took it into his head to be sociable, and, although it was a diversion, it was a grim one. He'd sit by my chair and look up at me with steady goose-berry eyes. His mistress whose adoring gaze hardly ever left him would cry: "Sit still, child! Don't move!" After an interval of holding his audience in suspense he'd land heavily on my lap and curl up, nose to tail. "Now don't touch him!" She'd remind me, for Tom didn't tolerate petting. So I'd sit there with my arms dangling at my sides while the mean old cat had a good nap. There was nothing I could do about the situation because in this house it was supposed to be an honor when Tom picked you out as a suitable lap.

The room we sat in was very sparsely furnished. The stove in the center was the focal point for a half-circle of chairs around it. Against one wall was an ordinary double bed, nearly always occupied by her son who lay with his long legs stretched out and one of his magazines in front of his face. He rarely joined in the conversation, but he was not an unfriendly person. When he leaned over to spit tobacco juice into the can beside his bed. he'd give us a friendly smile and a wink. I was so used to seeing him in this prone position that I had trouble recognizing him when I met him on the street.

This family's background was very different from the New York lady's. When they arrived in Silver they were already veterans of mining town life: they came from a town in Nevada which had suffered a "bust." After the death of the father, the mother had to support the family. She worked as a practical nurse, caring for the sick, assisting at births, laying out the dead. Sometimes she took a job as cook at a mine boarding house. At the time of our visits she was caring for the County's indigents,'who were no longer housed in the "Poor House" down the road but in a little house across the creek from hers. Her son kept the fire going there and she cooked meals and nursed the sick. This was the last stop for the old miners who could no longer manage for themselves in the little shacks they lived in. She was very conscientious about her job and very sympathetic with her charges. Often when we were there she would throw a little shawl around her shoulders and run across the creek to check on a sick patient.

Nearly all the stories we heard in this house had a macabre touch. She liked to tell about the last hours of dying people and she went into details about how she laid them out after they were dead. I couldn't help listening to every word of it but at the same time I wished I didn't have to hear it because I knew it would come back to haunt me at night. Her odd quirks and beliefs colored her stories. Forewarnings of disaster saved many from serious mishaps. Her dreams she told in great detail interpreting them from a "Dream Book" with a fancy cover which she kept on a high shelf, no doubt to keep it out of reach of children whom she always suspected of "thinking up mischief." Sister and I would have given anything for a peek at that book, but she never took it down in our presence.

One of her beliefs disturbed me so much that I learned to hate going to bed at night. She believed that many people had been misdiagnosed as dead when they were only in a deep sleep. As proof of this she cited the torn linings of caskets she had observed when bodies were exhumed, torn, she said, by the desperate finger nails of those who weren't really dead. I was so frightened by these stories that I was afraid to go to sleep at night for fear I might be mistakenly buried.

We were reluctant guests at this house not only because of the frightening stories we heard but because of some of our past experiences with her. Her back windows looked out on the long foot-bridge across the creek. We were not supposed to walk the railings when the creek was high but occasionally we felt we had to prove ourselves in front of other children. When she saw us she always yelled at us from her window and then made a point of telling Mamma about our transgressions. We resented her interference in our lives and we were not the only ones in town who sometimes felt that she was "interfering" in something that was none of her business. Once a man who was beating his horses to make them pull a heavy load in the snow was surprised when she flew out of her house and gave him a tongue lashing. She wouldn't leave him alone until he had unhitched the horses and reduced the load. Strangely her physical appearance was the opposite of threatening. She was small and slight. She wore old-fashioned calico dresses with pinched waists and full skirts. In repose she was a sweet little lady. In action she always reminded me of an ant because of her pinched waist and her hurrying-scurrying walk. She gave the impression that if she didn't get somewhere quickly something terrible would happen. I didn't know for a long time that she had once prevented something really terrible by taking it upon herself to interfere in a dangerous situation.

My father always spoke of her as "a great, great, lady" with a note of awe in his voice. The event he cited as proof took place when she was a cook at one of the mines. She had a young Chinese helper who had been given the name "Charlie" as was the custom in mining towns. Having their names changed was not by any means the worst indignity some of the them suffered. When the men at this mine discovered some personal items missing from the bunk house the thefts were naturally laid at the door of the standard scape-goat — Charlie. Having convinced themselves that he was the thief they decided to handle the matter in their own way. They kidnapped him and were in the act of lynching him when the cook missed her helper, and, immediately suspecting something from the talk she had heard among the men, set out to find him. When she came upon the victim, his captors were already stringing him up. By sheer force of her invective she made them cut him down and she revived him and saved his life.

When I was a child I had too many conflicting feelings about her to appreciate the courage of her action on this occasion and her other attempts to bring about justice and prevent cruelty. It wasn't until I was grown up that I realized that my father was right — she was a great lady.

CHAPTER IX

CHARACTERS

One of the "characters" who figured in the stories which were passed around by word of mouth was King Tan, or Pete as he was called in order to avoid such a difficult name. He became the last Chinese to live in Silver. He knew very well that his antics and jokes were often quoted, and I believe he gloried in the fact that he was considered a character. He had a building across from the Court-house which he used as a place of business and a home. It was an old two story structure which had once been a cheap hotel. A sign on it in an old photograph advertises "Beds 25¢ & 50¢." Another old photo-graph shows the sign not quite painted out and a smaller one hanging from the porch identifying it as a Chinese store. Some time later it became a saloon, for when Pete had his business there an ornate bar occupied one side of the room. Pete did not deal in drinks, though. In fact he did little business in the building itself which was a poorly stocked grocery. He bought meat from cattlemen who butchered steers occasionally, cut it up, and re-sold it. He also ordered vegeta-bles from Nampa. He had a small counter opposite the bar where he used an abacus to total up sums and weighed articles on a Chinese scale with brass pans. There was a small showcase on the same side of the room which had a few articles from China and could have been the stock of the former Chinese merchant. I can remember only one article in the case — a pair of tiny slippers which must have been intended for Chinese women with bound feet. I don't think Pete had any idea of selling these artifacts any more than he had for using the bar. In fact, he used the building infrequently as a store, except on the Fourth of July when he sold package after package of firecrackers. His idea of doing business was the traditional one of Chinese mer-chants in mining towns. He went around town with a couple of bas-kets on a pole across his shoulder and showed his wares at the homes of his customers. He may have continued this old-fashioned way of making sales partly because of his sociable nature, for once he was inside the door of a house he talked and talked. My mother resorted to a rather clever ruse for breaking off these long and often unintelligible conversations.

He recited over and over the contents of the baskets before he revealed them. After he'd made a sale he plunged into what he thought was our favorite topic of conversation — religion. He made this assumption because he, too, attended services at Our Lady of Tears, not as a member, but as an interested spectator. He didn't know, of course, that religion was a subject we tried to keep away from in our house. He liked to compare his religion to ours, emphasizing the tricky nature of the gods he was familiar with, how they liked to trip a person up, catch him off guard, and, if he didn't perform the proper acts of propitiation, punish him in some way. When it came to our religion he always ended his complimentary remarks with: "I like Jees Clist. He nice fella."

After he'd dealt with that subject to his satisfaction he filled us in on the news of the town. And then came the most unintelligible part of his discourse — the telling of jokes. He laughed before, during, and after telling them, working himself up to a state of near hysteria. It was then that Mamma would take up a dish towel and pretend to drive him out of the house by flapping it at him. He covered his head with his hands and shrieked joyously, as he picked up his baskets and trotted across the porch and down the path to the gate, laughing and dodging imaginary blows.

Pete was a thin, clean little man who negotiated Silver's rough streets with the agility of a cartoon rabbit. Another Chinese we often saw around town was a great contrast to him. Ah Moon did the dirty work of the town, cleaning toilets and disposing of garbage. He had also set another task for himself which horrified us. He spent hours digging up the bones in the Chinese cemetery behind our house for shipment to China. When he climbed our hill we avoided looking at him because he was a repulsive sight with his gray hair sticking out from his filthy hat, his eyes spotted with white dots, and his no-color clothes stiff with dirt. When we saw him coming across the foot bridge we'd run back and wait until he got across so we wouldn't have to meet him at close hand. When we told about these narrow escapes at home my father would sigh deeply and say: "Poor old fellow." He had a great sympathy with unfortunates and although he professed not to be a Christian he practiced the christian ethic to a greater degree than many who professed it. Often when he came home and saw Mamma's freshly baked bread and rolls displayed proudly on the kitchen table he would say: "Mamma, send the kids down to poor old Gibb with one of your loaves."

Gibb was probably second only to Ah Moon in the matter of dirt. But as a Welshman and a man from a famous mining country he was one of my father's favorites. We didn't object to the trip: in fact, we rather enjoyed having a look around his little shop to find some new detail of his housekeeping to horrify Mamma with when we came home. We'd find him sitting on his table working at mending an old coat or pants for someone, surrounded by dishes and cats. All the stray cats in town gravitated to Gibb's shop probably because of his lenient ways with them. Where else could a cat find a home where he was welcomed as an equal at the table? His cats were shy of strangers and when we walked in they vanished in waves toward the dark corners of the room. Once he showed us with pride a litter of kittens and offered to give us one. But we knew better than to accept because Mamma hated cats. The clean new little kittens seemed out of place in Gibb's dirty menage — as incongruous as the immaculate loaf of bread we set down in the midst of the clutter of his table.

Another character who was often quoted in town was our sheriff Mike Rock. He had first come to Silver in the early days as a miner and prospector. He rose in the profession to become a contractor who, with a crew of men, would run a tunnel or sink a shaft for an agreed amount of money per foot. It was while he was a mine contractor that he clashed with a man named Dewey, a promoter and developer of mines in the region. In the course of a brawl with Dewey he bit a diamond out of Dewey's shirt front and after pawning it in New York, returned to Ireland and married. He came back to Silver and raised a family there. At one time he was the town constable and at the same time a saloon keeper. Later he went into the cattle business down in sage-brush grazing lands of Owyhee County, and brought his cattle up to their summer grazing grounds around Silver. He was in the cattle business and had become a landlord for rented houses in the town when he was elected sheriff.

In old pictures of towns of the early West you often see men along main street leaning against posts. They leaned, of course, because the posts were there. Architecture has changed since that time so that we seldom see overhanging second story porches supported by posts and therefore we don't see men leaning. I sometimes think of it as a lost art. Some men lounged against a post, nudging it with one shoulder. Others barely touched it and crossed their legs so one boot toe rested on the ground at the far end of the other foot. That was a very casual pose. Some men leaned so long and so consistently against a post that it became theirs. Mike Rock had staked one out in front of the sheriff's office where he leaned with a dreamy look in his eyes while he probed at the teeth under his mustache with a tooth pick. His clothes were as careless as his pose — a hat of the sort a miner would wear underground, pulled down over his eyes, a shirt meant to be worn with a collar but lacking one, a vest that probably would have failed by inches if he had tried to button it, pants which miraculously did not fall off. He did not deign to speak to everyone who passed in front of him and if he caught our eye as we passed to buy an ice-cream cone at the drug store and gave us a wink, we felt flattered. He was a popular man but careless about putting himself out to be friendly.

If he was in the mood for talk he'd turn to a passerby and begin a monologue with the words: "By the hell now . . ." His Galway accent and his flair for telling a story usually drew others as they passed and before long he was off in full cry entertaining an audience.

His son Tom, who also had a gift for telling stories, told me the one I think expresses the fact that Mike took homage from friends as his natural lot in life. He had a tall handsome deputy from Cork whose devotion to him was legendary. Once when Mike was out of town Dave, the deputy, decided to surprise him with a gift when he came back. He was a fine carpenter. He had often heard Mike pine for the handy little carts of the old country, two wheeled, and built so that when an animal was unhitched from the shafts, it tipped backward and dumped its load. Dave used all his skills to make it balance correctly. He wanted to surprise Mike by making it the very image of the carts he had spoken of. But time was against him. He scoured the town for paint and all he could come up with was a vivid blue. He wanted to display the finished product so he painted it the day before Mike was expected back. When the great moment arrived for him to unveil his handiwork and savor his surprise Dave stood restlessly beside a silent Mike and waited while he thoughtfully probed his front teeth with the tooth pick. Finally Dave could bear the suspense no longer.

"Well," he burst out breathlessly. "What do you think?"

"And why," Mike demanded. "Couldn't you wait until I could get the green?"

Mike was not a big man but he was a scrappy fighter and liked to settle an argument with his fists. The legend of the fighting Irish may or may not be a valid generalization but I think it got encouragement in mining towns where people who did not have the courage to settle things in that manner themselves made heroes of those who did. My father was, as usual, an exception to the Irish prototype. He abhorred any kind of violence, although with his great strength and training as a boxer he could have laid out any man in town. A friend told me an incident about him many years after his death. It happened in a livery stable which was one of my father's favorite hangouts. Some young men in town had sent away for some boxing gloves and were jabbing away at each other in a haphazard fashion. Daddy couldn't restrain himself from giving them a few pointers and finally they persuaded him to take them on. "They couldn't lay a glove on him," my friend told me.

More than once Mike fought in the streets in a most unprofessional fashion. In my book "Gold Town or Ghost Town" I tell in some detail about the clash between W. H. Dewey and a German brewer which ended in a shooting match. Years later Mike clashed with another German brewer who was the last one to brew beer in Silver before the State went dry in 1916. The argument was over a bill Mike said he had paid and Fritz, the brewer, said he had not. They came to blows and the husky brewer soon had Mike flat on his back in the dust. Mike lost that one. He got up, recovered his hat, dusted himself off, and reached in his pocket and paid the bill. "You're a good man, Fritz," he said. After that incident Fritz became a member of the Mike Rock fan club.

On our trips to the Post Office or the stores we often saw a man who was not a leaner; his stance was so firm, so rock-like that it required no propping. Rudy was a small fair Italian from Northern Italy who had enough remarkable characteristics to make him the subject of many stories. He always stood in front of the leaners with his legs bowed out in back, two middle fingers of his hands thrust into the front pockets of his waist overalls, his nearly hairless huge white head shining in the sun like a piece of quartz. He projected the strength and immovability of a statue.

He had never learned much English. But he had a colorful vocabulary of four-letter words which men at that time used freely in each other's presence but never before women or children. Rudy hadn't learned to make this social distinction. He tried to pronounce his English in the Italian and French manner with the tongue against the front teeth and because *his* were gapped in front he ended up lisping in a peculiar way. This, of course, made him all the more quotable. He was cross-eyed, and had a wide smile which would have been charming except that the gap in his teeth prevented him from restraining the tobacco juice in his mouth. He was a regular fountain when he talked.

We thought of Rudy as more or less of a fixture in town. It didn't occur to us that he might have relatives until one day we got the surprising news that his wife, son, and daughter were coming to Silver. Sister and I had no opportunity to see them until our teacher announced one morning that she was expecting Rudy's children to arrive any minute. I don't know whether we expected them to be small statuettes resembling Rudy, but we had some preconceived ideas which turned out to be entirely wrong. When the teacher opened the door in answer to a timid knock we saw a grown up young lady of considerable beauty and a handsome young man. Anna, when introduced to us, smiled around the room with obvious joy, showing off a perfect set of teeth. Her brother glanced at his surroundings with a flash of blue eyes and a cynical smile which said plainly: "You call this dump a school?" We found out later that these attractive people came from the large city of Turin and if we were surprised at them, they were even more surprised at us.

However, Anna spent the year in school with her much younger fellow students, picking up English quickly, beguiling us with her beautiful smile, and filling us in on the facts of life. Her brother whose name was Enrico (which was quickly changed to Rich) stayed in school only a few days. He always looked down at his humble desk before he sat down at it, in a condescending manner as if to say, "This is ridiculous." One day he disappeared. I don't mean that he went away. He became a miner and joined the men who walked up and down the trails to the mines, indistinguishable from each other because of the white muck that sprayed their faces and clothes underground. For though our mountains were green and gray and brown on the outside the rock blasted out of them was often white. If we recognized Rich at all after he became a miner it would have been because of the unusual blue of his eyes. In the few glimpses we got of his mother we saw that she had them, too, along with Anna's fine teeth, and a head of thick silvery hair.

One day we heard that Anna had left town. Then we heard that she was in California. Shortly after that Rich and his mother went, too. Rudy took to standing around the streets again. He did not seem any different than he was before his family had come and gone. He did not talk about them. He continued to be a character whose expressions were quoted by way of entertainment. One of the anecdotes concerned a man who was always pulling samples of ore out of his pocket and holding them under somebody's nose while he challenged them with "What does that look like?" The answer he was looking for was: that looks like Morning Star ore, or Trade Dollar ore, or the ore of some other famously rich mine. But the correct answer was usually not supplied so he'd say: "It looks like Morning Star ore, doesn't it? Doesn't it?" It was, of course, a piece of ore from a mine of his that he was trying to sell. Once when Rudy was standing in his fixed position in front of the leaners this man came up and thrust one of his samples under Rudy's nose. "What does that look like, Rudy?" he demanded. Rudy didn't make a move to take it but just stood stolidly looking down at it. Finally he raised his wild eyes, smiled broadly, and said: "It look like chicken thit!"

CHAPTER X

THE DEATH OF THE BEEKEEPER

In the summer or fall when District Court was in session in our town Sister and I were always eager to find a pretext for crossing the creek to take in the strange sight of our main streets crowded with cars, of people dressed in city clothes hurrying back and forth from the Courthouse to the Hotel, of the bailiff herding the jury toward the hotel dining room for meals. We looked on the scene with pride and wonder as Silver was suddenly transformed in our eyes into a metropolis. Sometimes Daddy was among the jurors and even his familiar figure looked strange in a suit, a white shirt, and a tie. As we walked up and down the main streets we silently counted the cars and then compared our figures as we turned toward home across the long foot bridge. "Thirty two!" I'd say. "Thirty three!" Sister would correct me triumphantly. "You forgot to count the stage!"

We knew there were prisoners in the jail behind the sheriff's office in the Courthouse because we had a contact who worked there and kept us informed. Those who were there for capital crimes were the ones who interested us most for those were the ones the town talked about. Prisoners often had to stay over the winter in our jail because travel was too inconvenient in the snowy season for the court to meet there. Sometimes prisoners were there for such a long period that the attitude of the town changed completely toward them as the months went on. That was the case involving a naturopath in one of the valley towns who had shot and killed an eighteen year old neighbor who was out on a lark with his girl. The young couple had parked their car near the naturopath's watermelon patch and the young man had gone over the fence with the intention of taking a melon, so the naturopath believed. He blasted away at him with a shot gun, wounding him so gravely that he died the next day. When he first came to the jail that fall to await trial the next summer, the naturopath did not receive much sympathy from the residents of the town. He was a mean old man who had killed a very young man over a matter of slight importance, the kind of lark that many young people had engaged in themselves. But during the winter a flu epidemic struck Silver and the naturopath in jail was the nearest thing to a doctor in town. He was credited with saving the life of a mother of a large family whose illness had kept her in delirium from fever. He suggested that they immerse her in cool water and the treatment brought her fever down. When she recovered, the naturopath's stock went up considerably: he was no longer a mean old man. He was lovable Doc Smith who had saved a life. The changed attitude toward him may have had something to do with the fact that he was acquitted in the summer.

Another prisoner, F. A. Young, spent nearly two years in our jail. His escape on a Sunday morning in May when the mountains were still packed with snow brought some of the excitement and some of the tragedy of the early days to Silver in the 1920s. I was nine years old when Young, a farmer and beekeeper from Grandview — a town on the Snake River — came to Silver in custody of the sheriff for killing a man named Fones whom he had employed to help him with his bee business. I had forgotten the details of the crime so I went to the Courthouse a few years ago to read the record of the preliminary hearing for Young.[1]

He testified that he had hired L. C. Fones three months before the shooting to help him with the bees. The agreement between the two men was that Fones could take his choice between wages for his work or ten percent of the money from the sale of honey. Although Fones kept demanding more money because, he claimed, he was increasing the production of the bees, Young claimed that production had actually fallen. The root of the trouble between the two men seems to have been that Fones considered himself an equal partner with Young and, in fact, the greater expert in the matter of bees, while Young regarded him merely as an employee. Young said that Fones refused to do the work of extracting the honey from the hives, at the time Young considered extraction necessary, and when Young started to do it himself Fones said to him: "You put that honey back in the hives and do it damn quick. There is going to be something doing around here if you don't." He testified that he put the honey back because he was afraid of Fones. Young quoted him as saying on another occasion "Old man, I will get you if you don't watch out." At other times Fones called him "Dad" — an odd salutation for a man who was only twelve years older than he was.

Young said that he had tried to fire Fones and had put his 'grip' and bedding out of the little house he had given him to live in on the farm. But when Fones ordered him to put the things back he did so. He then gave Fones written orders to get off the place but that had no effect either. He then tried to get Fones put under bond to keep the peace. When he did not succeed in doing so he consulted his lawyer. If Young was telling the truth about what the lawyer told him, he got incredibly bad advice: the lawyer advised him to "heel himself" — an old expression meaning to carry a gun. He borrowed a gun from a friend but he did not tell him the real reason for wanting it. He said it was to shoot dogs with.

Fones had also borrowed a gun which he told the owner he intended to shoot bee birds with. No gun was found on Fones body at the time of his death.

Two other witnesses testified at the hearing that Fones had made threats against Young. One of them related an incident about the two men which indicated unreasonableness on the part of Fones. Young was driving his car one day when he slid into a ditch. Fones, who was driving Young's truck, refused to pull him out because it was Sunday. Other witnesses testified that Fones had bragged to them that he came from "fighting stock" and that when he had been on a police force somewhere he had killed two or three men. He said that he could kill a man with a blow of his fist.

The confrontation between the two men came on September 15th, 1920 when Fones drove up as Young was working with the bees. Young testified that as Fones drove toward him he yelled: "Lee, for God's sake stop!" When he ignored the order Young fired at him three times. Fones was wounded twice in the left temple and once in the sternum. There wasn't much doubt that the shots were meant to kill. But perhaps the thing that damaged Young most in his testimony at the hearing is what he did after he shot the man. He testified that he finished his work with the bees before he even checked to see about Fones. Then he went and turned himself in to the justice of the peace.

Young spent the next nine months in jail in Silver awaiting trial. On the 10th of June, 1921, Judge Raymond L. Givens came from Boise to hear this and other cases of the third district court. It was not a case that attracted much attention in the Boise press and even the Silver City Avalanche had little to say about it. The Statesman[2] in Boise ran two brief stories on it on the 15th and 17th of June. The first stated that a jury had been empaneled and one witness for the prosecution heard. Several witnesses for the defense would be heard, it said. By the time the second Statesman story appeared on the 17th, Young had been convicted of second degree murder. The jury was out about three hours. The penalty for the crime would be not less than 10 or more than 20 years. The Avalanche[3] account of the trial added little to this. The newspaper was a weekly and by the time it came out the news of the trial was already well known.

Young stayed on in the Silver City jail for almost another year. His bond had been set at $5,000, which doesn't seem like a great sum to us now. It was a lot of money in those days. However the man had a farm and other assets which would seem valuable enough to raise such a sum. He had been given time to file an appeal to the State Supreme Court by March 1, 1922. Before word of the appeal or the bond reached him Young decided to take matters into his own hands.

News of the events of that Sunday morning, May 7th, 1922, spread rapidly around town. An eye witness who had seen Young walk away from the Courthouse told us that he had assumed that Young had finally raised his bond money. We heard how the discovery of the escape was made when a citizen heard old Jim Murray, the jailer, shouting and beating on tin pans. We heard that the sheriff had been summoned back from a town a hundred miles away and his deputy recalled from another section of the County. And we heard that when the officers returned they formed a posse of men on horseback to pursue the escapee, who, by this time, had an eight hour start on them. And finally by late afternoon we heard the tragic end of the story.

One would have to go back to the history of the early days of this town to match the excitement Young's escape caused. Those who had had a part in it, whether as eye witnesses or mere observers, gladly rehearsed its details time after time. And people who had had no part in it at all found an audience for their accounts of exactly what they were doing at the time they heard the news. My family had no involvement but we felt its effects just the same. My father was always depressed by acts of violence and we were inclined to take our cue for behavior from him. For me there was another disillusionment. I had assumed up to that time that nothing but the literal truth ever found its way into newspapers. I found out how wrong that assumption was when I read the account of Young's escape in the Boise paper the next day. Recently I went back and reread the account, looked up the story in another Boise paper, and found the story in our local paper as well. The Idaho Daily Statesman[4] featured the story on the front page under the headline: SLAYER TAKES OWN LIFE WHEN RUN TO EARTH. Under the sub-head FRED W. (sic) YOUNG DIES BY HIS OWN HAND WHEN CORNERED IN FIGHT AFTER DARING ESCAPE FROM OWYHEE COUNTY JAIL, the story supplied details which must have come from someone who was badly misinformed about the incident or from a reporter with a vivid imagination. Young was said to have "sprung" at Sheriff Pearman (who was one hundred miles away) when he opened the door of the cell, overpowering him, and locking him in the cell. He then made his escape with a bag of provisions he had hoarded. The other newspaper in Boise at the time — the Evening Capital News[5] made an even better story of its saying that Pearman was attacked by two prisoners who took his gun and locked him up. The second escapee is not mentioned in the story again. "As soon as he (the sheriff) could arouse help from the outside," the story goes on, "a posse was formed and took up Young's track." If things had moved as fast as this story implies the whole affair would have been over by ten o'clock that morning. It was not until four in the afternoon that Young was sighted less than two miles from town.

The Owyhee Avalanche[6] came out on Friday so its story was nearly a week old. It is essentially the same story I remember hearing at the time:

Attempted Get-Away
Prisoner Escapes And Is Shot By Sheriff's Posse

"Fred L. (sic) Young, under sentence of ten to twenty years for second degree murder committed in September 1920, was shot to death by a sheriff's posse about a mile below town last Sunday afternoon.

"In the morning at about 7:30 when the jailer, James Murray, went into the jail as was his regular custom, to get water for his morning ablutions, Young who slept in the main room, was in his bed apparently asleep. Passing into the washroom Murray observed an old shirt in the toilet and stepped back to demand an explanation. He was just in time to see Young going out with a pack, an overcoat and a hat, the latter the property of his fellow prisoner. The pack contained a generous supply of provisions taken from the prison larder, the prisoners preparing their own meals. Murray rushed for the door but was too late to prevent the bolt being slipped from the outside.

"Young then went into the jailer's bedroom, appropriated a gun, broke the crank off the telephone, and walked out, leaving a note on the sheriff's desk. As he walked down the street he passed John Hawes and Dave O'Neil, who were waiting in front of the telephone office for volunteer workers to assemble. They said, "Well, old Young got his bond at last," and paid no further attention. Shortly thereafter these two decided to go on to the snow banks. Just below town they saw Young abroad on the road and observed him step behind the powder house until they passed by.

"Prosecuting attorney Wright A. Stacy had left Hawes and O'Neil in front of the telephone office and two minutes before gone to round up other workers. Thus tragedy No. 1 was avoided as the attorney would have realized the situation and attempted to apprehend the desperate man, who according to the other occupant of the jail, had expressed his desire to kill the prosecuting attorney and the deputy sheriff — and he was a good shot.

"Meanwhile the imprisoned jailer was beating tin pans and making all noise possible, finally attracting the attention of John Hailey who released him from his plight and the alarm was given.

"A posse was soon out looking for the escaped murderer but it was not until about four o'clock that he was seen coming out of the brush near the K. P. cemetery.

"Herb Bonnell and Miss Edna Grete, out for a walk, were first to see him, coming directly toward them. Directing his companion to a place of safety, Herb thought to speak with the man and induce him to surrender. However, unarmed and realizing his defensive position, he took the wiser course, stepped behind some rocks and signalled the sheriff's party who had assembled at the old poor house for consultation.

"Steadily advancing and appealing to the man to give up his gun the sheriff was less than fifty feet from him when Young began firing, one bullet going through the rim of Mr. Pearman's hat. The affair was soon over.

"Young, who was slightly below the officers, fired three shots and as the trend of the fatal bullet was upward, it was thought possible he fired it himself. That, however, is immaterial.

"Coroner Dr. Erkenbeck came from Grandview and held an inquest, the jury determining that the man met his death at the hands of the posse and himself.

"The body was sent to Mountain Home for burial.

"Neither the sheriff nor his deputy were in town at the time of the murderer's escape. The former was at Grandview on Saturday looking after parties to a shooting scrape and the latter was returning via Murphy from an official visit to the western border of the County. Both were due that evening but made a rush trip when notified."

The Statesman had closed its story by noting that Young was from a well-known pioneer family and that his father had been the contractor who built the old Overland Hotel, a famous inn of pioneer days. A quote from Young's lawyer, K. I. Perky of Boise, stated: "No doubt Young was insane, but his insanity was not heriditary. His family was exceedingly prominent in the early days in both Idaho and Oregon." This curious statement was designed, I guess, to leave untarnished the reputations of those pioneers.

Another point on which the Boise paper's account differed from the Avalanche's was the matter of who fired the first shot. The Statesman had the posse firing in the direction of Young before he fired at them.

Another item in the Avalanche that day was a copy of the note Young left on the sheriff's desk. It said:

"Sunday Morning, May 7, 1922
R. L. McDonnell. (the Deputy Sheriff)
Dear Sir:

"I received word day before yesterday that a friend would be waiting for me down the road toward Murphy this morning with a saddle horse to take me to the railroad the other side of Murphy if I wanted to go. Now Bob on account of this long confinement I am just about all in and for some unknown reason my bond has failed to materialize.

"If I stay I won't last long. It's a case of death sure. So just as well die out as in. Now I would ask that you do not try to find me or telephone to the outside, but let me go and I will be very far away where you will never find me again. By the time you receive this I will be far away and going strong. I will keep out of sight so no one will see me, to burden you or Roy (the sheriff). I hated to and did not want to make this move, but I am sick and liable to die any time so I had to do something."

The letter is curiously polite and also naive. How could a prisoner believe that his appeal to the deputy sheriff to ignore his escape would be honored? And why does he address it to McDonnell, the man the other prisoner maintained he wanted to kill? The tone of the letter is friendly, apologetic, pitiful. It speaks less of insanity than it does of desperation.

Did he really have a confederate who was going to help him get away? I don't remember hearing anything about that subject and I have found no record of it. In fact I have been unable to find any record in the county courthouse of this stirring event — the escape and death of F. A. Young.

As is usual in a small town where few exciting things happen this event was the subject of conversation for a long time. There are always people who like to believe that they escaped by the skin of their teeth from a threatening situation: there were some here who believed that Young, the escaped murderer loose in the hills, had been a danger to all of us. But I think most of us were appalled and sickened by the incident. Despair is a sad condition and despair was written all over that pitiful note. "So just as well die out as in," he had written.

CHAPTER XI

THE LONG WINTER

Every year when we went back to school we found more empty desks. As children grew up their parents moved away because there was no high school in Silver. And then too, as the mines closed, miners left to look for work in other mining towns. Occasionally we were surprised to find "new kids" whose families moved into Silver when out-lying country schools in the county closed. In 1921 this delightful surprise awaited us: a new girl and boy of our ages took their places at two of the empty desks. But after a few days we didn't see them again for two weeks. When they came back they were pale and thin and the girl showed us a strange after-effect of their illness — the skin on her fingers was peeling off.

A short while later I had to stay at home with what Mamma thought was one of my frequent sore throats. My health had always caused more concern than Sister's because I was small and thin and had a poor appetite. Mamma scolded and Daddy joked about the fact that a few bites of a meal seemed to satisfy me. "Is that all you're going to eat?" Mamma would ask despairingly. "Dude," Daddy would say. "If you don't eat your dinner you won't grow up to be good-lookin' like I am."

My sore throat persisted and my fever rose so high that I became delirious. I can remember the confusion of my thoughts very well. I thought I was a character in a book I had been reading and the danger that character was in from the villain was my own danger. I tried desperately to escape from her perils. Mamma became even more worried when she saw that I was breaking out in a red rash all over. She sent Sister to a neighbor's house to borrow a "doctor" book. It was pretty plain from the symptoms described in it that I had scarlet fever. I stayed in bed for another week or so and then recovered without any treatment. By that time Sister began showing signs of the disease.

Mamma was encouraged by my quick recovery and no doubt

thought that Sister, the big strong girl of the family, the one who always ate her meals and asked for more, would soon be out of bed and back in school. But, as the winter closed in on us, bringing day after day of steady snow fall, it was soon apparent that she was very ill. Our lives in the snug little house changed drastically during the next few months. The front bedroom became the sick room. Mamma and Daddy slept on a borrowed cot in the front room and I was more or less confined to our little back bedroom-dining room. I wasn't allowed to go back to school for fear of spreading the contagion to others and when I say that I was "confined" I mean it literally, for every time I ventured out into the kitchen or front part of the house I was told to keep out of the way. Mamma's friend, the lady from Nevada, was helping out and she had no patience at all with me, warning me frequently not to be "underfoot." I, who had gained so much attention with my poor eating habits, could now announce loudly that I was hungry and be utterly ignored. I learned to fix my own meals and my appetite improved remarkably.

I could never be sure when I woke up whether it was day or night, for hurrying feet made the trip from bedside to kitchen all night and the electric lights we had always been so careful to conserve burned all the time. Daddy was as quiet as it was possible for him to be. He still banged the stove lids but rarely sang. Sometimes he shouted a few words and was promptly cut off by a stern "Shhhh!" from Mamma's helper.

After Daddy went to work I was the only one in the house who was free to go on errands and I prayed every day that something would be needed from the drugstore or grocery store. It was a great relief to get out of the house for a few minutes. I had to ski because the snow was so heavy that winter that paths filled up overnight. The town was very strange looking. Besides the snow that fell, the accumulation on roofs was dumped into the streets, for there was no other place to put it. Two story buildings had snow up to the level of second story porches. One story buildings like the post office had a little pointed gable above the drifts. I enjoyed the strange appearance of the place and I never failed to take advantage of another attraction in front of the Courthouse: some ambitious boys had dug a tunnel through the big pile of snow there and I could walk through it from the general store to the drugstore.

It was hard to entertain myself in that little back room when I was so used to Sister's company. Even when we read we often said: "Listen to this," and read something aloud that we thought remarkable. Now I couldn't get books from the school library so I had to content myself with what we had at home. Someone had given us "The Arabian Nights" in an edition with a colorful cover. But every time we set out to read it we were put off by the terrible print on the cheap pages. Some of the words were a blur. In my desperation for something new to read I began to decipher it, guessing at words I couldn't make out. The tales were worth the effort and, as Scheherazade saved the lives in the Sultan's harem with her tales, I saved my sanity by becoming absorbed in them. Another book which had already seen much hard wear was a book of poems sent by an aunt. It was called "Golden Numbers" and I can still see those golden letters on its red cover. It was an anthology of some of the best English and American poetry. Sister and I had learned many of them "by heart" and even incorporated them into our games. Two which we loved to chant were "The Raven" and "The Bells." To pass the time in my grim isolation I memorized many more. Years later when I started to college, a teacher who was curious about how much her students knew, brought some quotations from famous poems to class. I could identify nearly all of them. Since no one else in the class knew them she became curious about me and stopped me after class to ask how I knew so much poetry. I was too shy to tell her about the hours I spent in that little back room in a snowed-in mining town, so I just said that I read a lot.

Because of the deep snow that winter the stage was very often late and sometimes had to turn back before it reached Silver. A neighbor brought our mail when he got his, so I didn't get to go out on that errand. As the weather became worse Sister grew weaker. When she began having hemorrhages Mamma sent word to our telephone operator to find a doctor. The doctors in Nampa and Boise didn't want to come because of the uncertainty of getting back out to their practices. But a doctor in Jordan Valley, Oregon, Dr. Jones, was used to calls from outlying places and always made it a point to answer them even if it meant risking his own health. He managed to get as far as Delamar where a friend of Daddy's met him with a horse which he rode the nine miles up the creek. His face was red from the cold when he came to our door and, as he took off his big fur-lined gloves Daddy put a stiff drink he had just poured from a bottle of Canadian whiskey which had somehow crossed the 49th parallel and arrived at our remote village, into his hands.

He was not encouraging about Sister's chances for recovery. The hemorrhages had left her so weak that she had to have a stimulant for her heart. He also left some powders whose purpose I have forgotten. These were the pre-pill days, at least for us in the far West, and doctors and druggists handed out little paper-wrapped doses of medicines which were dissolved in water. The lady from Nevada took the preparation of Sister's doses so seriously that she insisted that I be excluded from the kitchen while she prepared them. She told Mamma that I "got on her nerves." The doctor examined me and pronounced me healthy which surprised Mamma since she could not quite give up the idea that my eating habits were nearly fatal.

In spite of the rough journey he'd had the doctor assured us that he would come back in two weeks to check on her progress. He talked to Mamma and Daddy for a long time before he left. I wasn't allowed to hear the conversation, but I guessed its seriousness by the fact that an air of gloom settled on the household after he left.

Not long after his visit, the priest arrived from Nampa. I didn't know he was coming until I was summoned from the little back room and taken into the sick room. It was the first time I had been in the room and I was shocked at the sight of Sister whose matted hair had been cut off close to her head and whose lips looked black in her white face. She looked like a very sick old man. Candles were burning on the dresser and the priest was preparing to administer Holy Communion. I was told to lie down on the bed beside Sister and we both received the Host. Then the priest turned again to the dresser and mixed something in a small dish. He approached the bed and dipping his fingers in the mixture began annointing Sister's forehead, hands, and feet. I realized then that he was giving her the last rites, which we had read about in our catechism, but had never thought would apply to us.

The days dragged on. Mamma and her helper held many low toned conferences in the kitchen. Should they be hopeful or less so about some new development in Sister's illness? They couldn't decide. But on his next visit Dr. Jones was more encouraging. The hemorrhages had stopped and he believed now that she might make it. He instructed Mamma and her helper about how her convalescence should proceed and the kind of diet she should have. He told them that her muscles would be so weak that she would have to learn to walk again. Her diet included plenty of fresh fruit, which was pretty hard to come by in our snowed-in town. However when Mamma wrote to our grandmother about the problem she sent a case of oranges and grapefruit which arrived in good condition on the stage. At that time grapefruit was just beginning to make its appearance on the market. It was entirely new to Silver. Mamma had read about it in magazines and knew how to prepare it. Visitors who now dropped in to inquire about Sister sometimes asked to see the grapefruit, its fame having spread around the town, due in no little part, I think, from my bragging about it at school.

It was a great relief to me to escape from the confinement of my little room and go back to school. I was still not allowed to have much contact with Sister because Mamma's helper was around alleging that I was a disruptive influence, but every morning when I left the house I walked along the porch past the window of the sick room where I could make signs to her and mouth words which she seemed to understand. To me she looked even worse than the night I had seen her receive the last rites. Most of her hair had come out and she was terribly thin. One morning as I pantomined something to her she gasped and closed her eyes tightly and seemed to be in pain. I was about to run back and alert Mamma when she opened her eyes and I saw that they were bright and shining: she had been trying to laugh and she was so weak it hurt.

Mama began getting her up every day, first to stand on her wobbly legs and then to take a few steps. One day when I came home from school she was sitting in a chair wrapped in a blanket. She had to go back to bed almost at once because she had insisted on staying up until I came and was very tired.

Another wonderful present arrived in the mail for her — a blue corduroy bathrobe trimmed in fur and lined with China silk. Neither of us had ever owned a bathrobe and we hadn't even aspired to such a luxurious garment. I was more than a little jealous but I compensated for it by talking it up at school as I had talked up the grapefruit. Before long Mamma let me bring one of Sister's friends at a time to see her and to get a glimpse of the wonders I had described — the grapefruit and the bathrobe. When I came home from school with one of the girls we would find Sister sitting in the front room in her majestic robe with a little lace cap on her head to hide her baldness. She made a charming invalid with her pale face and bright blue eyes.

Her long illness had changed all of us. Daddy was a bit quieter, Mamma transferred her worries to Sister, and Sister was no longer a child. She talked like a grown-up about her illness with Mamma's friends and she no longer sat on the floor or played with paper dolls. She crocheted and embroidered like a real lady and after she recovered she became interested in cooking and recipes. It was the end of the intimacy of our childhood.

I had changed, too, although I wasn't conscious of it right away. I knew that Sister was a different person now, but I couldn't join her yet in that grown-up world. My confinement in the little back room had made a serious reader out of me. I began reading books which Mamma said were "too old" for me. I read some of Poe's stories and Hawthorne's and I found some books on a shelf in the school room which hadn't been disturbed for years — exciting tales of two rivals, Hector and Achilles. Later I learned that I had been reading one of the world's classics. The little library upstairs in the schoolhouse was about the size of a large clothes closet. It had some very good books in it, some of which were probably meant for the high-school that had once been up on the second story. When I started to college I found that I had read all the books English Literature teachers hope you have read by the time you get there. And most of them came from that library which was the size of a clothes closet.

Although I read a lot I still played like a child and I was still quite capable of "getting on people's nerves." Sister and I had always been different in that she was more cautious about offending people. Her teachers considered her an ideal student. Some of mine disliked me for my liveliness and lack of respect for authority. We were both good students but I was apt to rush through an assignment so I could read something on my own. Occasionally I wrote poems in the back of my notebook. Few of them were serious. They were often parodies of songs or poems. One of my teachers was rather shocked at a parody I had written of a sentimental song which inadvertently fell into her hands. But another teacher was impressed when I wrote a description of a snow storm. I don't know what I said about the subject, but at least I picked out one that I had experienced.

Every year but one when we went back to school we were greeted by a new teacher. The reason for this was that the teachers were usually from "the outside," and one winter in this isolated snowy mountain town was enough for them. The one exception was when our teacher was a local girl and, in my opinion, the best one we ever had. She taught for two years before she married and moved away. The other teachers came to Silver either because they lacked experience or they were too old or had some infirmity such as deafness. One died in the middle of the year. The prosecuting attorney's wife was a licensed teacher and she completed the year although she was expecting a child. The grades were divided between two rooms, four grades in each. At that time examinations were given by the State to students in the seventh and eighth grades. I don't remember an incidence of anyone in my room failing to pass. I do remember that I found an error on the reading examination where a quotation attributed to Ruskin was written by Francis Bacon. I pointed it out in my answer. I may have lost a few points on my reading score because of my presumption.

The one-room school (two, in this case) has probably been given more credit than it deserves by those who look back at it through the rose-colored glasses of nostalgia. There was a greater intimacy in a situation where everybody knew everybody else and it is sometimes supposed that the teacher was able to give much more individual attention. But a teacher trying to teach five or six subjects to several grades did not have time for much such attention. Besides, children are probably already motivated before they start to school about how they will perform as students and the school situation is not as important as we make out. In our case Sister and I were motivated by my father's inquiring mind and the tradition of reading in my mother's family.

CHAPTER XII

ALGIA

The last syllable of the word nostalgia is the Greek word for pain — *algia*. My old unabridged dictionary defines it simply as "homesickness," but it has come to mean more than that. Another more recent dictionary defines it as "a wistful yearning for something past or irrecoverable." Sometimes that yearning is translated into what might be called "the good old days syndrome." As we get older new ideas and new inventions make the world stranger and stranger, and we tend to turn to the past for comfort. All its little familarities, even its miseries, turn out to have some redeeming feature that was really, after all, good for us. We worked from dawn to dusk, but that shaped our characters for the struggle ahead. We lived in poorly heated houses, wore inadequate clothing, and subsisted on poor diets, but look how it all turned out. Today we are ourselves, tested in the crucible of experience, while the present generation, shamelessly spoiled and indulged, goes on with its grasshopper existence.

The good old days were, in fact, very much like the present — both good and bad. That wistful yearning is comforting but if we look closer we remember the *algia*. What I am going to write about now has more pain than yearning. Fortunately the misery of our last year in Silver has not blotted out for me the joys of growing up in the intimacy of a small town, of living close to nature, of treasuring a lot of fine memories.

My sister and I were fortunate in that we had kind and loving parents who rarely punished us and never mistreated us. I have described my father as a hearty, cheerful, interesting, man whose company we delighted in. He would no doubt be tagged with one of today's labels as an "outgoing" or "warm" personality. But such labels often deal with only the superficial aspects a casual observer sees. Most of us are a lot more complicated than the image we project in social situations. My father was such a person. To understand him I would have to go back to his beginnings in Ireland and his youth in

Missouri. Unfortunately, he always avoided, whenever he could, any discussion of his past.

We knew that his mother had come to this country as a widow with five children and settled on a farm in Missouri. He had an uncle who either came with them or was already here. I don't know whether he was the mother's brother or the father's. He died before my father came out west. His mother and sister moved to California and he must have kept in touch with them to some extent because we sometimes got letters from the sister when we lived in Silver. I will never forget the appearance of one of those letters. I had heard about the custom of sending a letter edged in black to communicate bad news. There is a melodramatic song on the subject and it may have been one that my father sang during his fire-lighting rites. When Daddy opened the black-edged letter he looked stricken and quickly left the house. I don't remember him discussing his mother's death. I asked him many times about his father and the most I could get out of him was a sigh and: "Oh . . . he died." He did not want to talk about any subject that had caused him pain and he tried to put as much distance as he could between himself and the painful experience.

I think he enjoyed our outings in the mountains as much as we did. He taught us to observe birds and other animals, rock formations and what they revealed about the way mountains were formed, minerals and crystal formations in rocks. And he always pointed out the famous old mines and told us what he knew about them. We followed him into mines and he explained his work to us as if we were adults. We learned that you called the area you drilled into in a tunnel "the face," we knew what a stope was, a hanging wall and a foot wall. We went into mills with him where the thundering stamps were crushing the ore. We saw the copper plates moving back and forth to make the heavy metal sink to the bottom. He explained the process to us in serious tones. When he brought home samples of rock from his claims we filled an old wash tub with water in the back yard while he pounded up the rock in a small hand mortar. We waited eagerly while he panned out the fine powder in his gold pan, swishing it back and forth in the tub, and we examined the fine streak of minerals with him — the black silver and the shiny gold specks.

He had another trait that set him apart from most of the people he came in contact with: he was interested in theories. He liked to speculate about how the earth and other planets were formed, how religions originated, where ideas came from. His speculations sometimes met with embarrassment on the part of those who thought they already had the answers to such questions or indifference from those who didn't want to think about such things. He was poorly educated. Instead of learning a trade when he was a young man he should have done something that was more of a challenge intellectually. When he heard those lectures on geology in Wyoming he came in contact with a subject that really interested him. He tried to put what he had learned there to the test of experience when he came to the Owyhee country as a prospector in the '90's, but he had picked a mining area that had already seen its great days and was coming to the end of its second period of prosperity.

While we were still quite young we knew that family life bored him. He would come home from work covered with the white muck of the mines and declaring with every breath how tired he was. I don't doubt that he was tired for the work was hard and he had to walk "to and fro," as the Cornishmen said. But after a bath in the wash tub, a change of clothes, and a hearty dinner, he miraculously revived, and after sitting down for a moment in the front room, he'd jump up and say: "Well, I guess I'll walk down and see what's going on in town." He spent his evenings either at one of the livery stables or the hotel barroom where he played cards.

The livery stables took the place of a men's club in a town like Silver. Men gathered in a little room that was used for an office or a place for keeping harness and other supplies. I can remember an evening when we were quite small and Daddy was charged with taking care of us for some reason. He took us to a livery stable on the street along Jordan Creek. We sat in a little room where the walls were covered with calendars and the smell of hay was overpowering. A jolly man named Jack Hunt was in charge of the place and he seemed delighted to have company. We walked with him and Daddy down the length of the barn behind the huge haunches and switching tails of the horses as they stood chewing and snorting and stamping in their stalls. Daddy loved horses and even talking about them was a pleasure to him.

When he was not working he spent a lot of time playing cards in the barroom of the hotel. Mamma often had to send us down to tell him to come home for supper. I liked going into the barroom because it gave me a chance to look at the pictures on the walls. There were two huge scenes of trotting races with the drivers in bright costumes, and a dark picture of men on a train playing cards on the top of a beaver hat. In the winter the barroom was closed and we would find him in the lobby of the hotel talking mining with the old fellows who hung around the big stove.

I don't remember that Mamma ever argued with him about the evenings he spent away from home. She read or worked on sewing or mending while we played. It wasn't considered odd in our town for men to seek out men's company in the evenings, but it was not the general practice either, for if it had been the meager facilities of the hotel and livery stables would have been overcrowded. In the days when the saloons were open I suppose these same men who met to talk or play cards would have spent their time in saloons. It's possible that "moonshine" sometimes provided refreshment for these gatherings, but I don't think it could have been the attraction for my father who was a modest drinker, if he drank at all. Because of the taboos of the time concerning the use of "bad" language and conversation about sex in the presence of "respectable" women, these men enjoyed the freedom that their all-male meetings provided. There were still lodges for men in town but the women's lodges had disbanded, for reasons I am not aware of. Daddy did not belong to any of the men's lodges and the only organization I am sure he belonged to was the Western Federation of Miners which was no longer active in Silver.

He had finished a contract at a mine on the east side of War Eagle Mountain in 1924 when he met a former resident of Silver who had come to town looking for mines to promote and sell stock in. This man did not have a good reputation in town and Daddy was naive enough about people to trust him. During the summer he brought many prospective stockholders in to look at Daddy's claims and others on the mountain. I don't know the details of what happened in the course of this affair but I know that it ended with the loss of his claims. It must have been a very bad blow for him because he had invested such great hopes in them and, in spite of how much other bad luck he had, there was always the possibility that he might strike it rich one summer. It may have seemed like a slim hope to more practical people, but it was one that no doubt sustained him for many years. The situation of the veins of ore on that mountain encouraged many men to cling to their claims there, for the big veins of the early days had disappeared in a rather mysterious manner. In mining countries of similar formations such as the Comstock in Virginia City, Nevada, the first harvest of gold near the surface was followed by a period of decline, and then, as deeper penetrations continued, even greater wealth was uncovered. Because of many faults and fractures in the veins on War Eagle it was difficult to trace them. The ore gave out as shafts went deeper and tunnels cut veins at different depths. Somewhere in that mountain, many people came to believe, there must be continuations of those first rich veins. So it wasn't an entirely ridiculous hope that some lucky miner might happen on to sudden wealth.

I think my father reacted as he had reacted in the past to matters that disturbed him: he tried to put as much distance between himself and the troubling thoughts as he could. He decided to go to the Boise Basin to look for work. Neither he nor Mamma made much of his departure. We knew that he planned to go out on the stage on a certain morning that summer and I was half awake when I heard him say to Mamma in the kitchen: "No, don't wake them." I think this was another indication of his reluctance to face a painful scene. I heard him close the front door and walk across the porch. He started to whistle as he closed the gate.

We heard from one of Mamma's brothers shortly after that saying that he had stopped to see them, but we heard nothing from him. As the days turned into weeks, Sister and I came to dread making our trips to the Post Office for the mail. When we came home time after time empty handed we had to witness the keen disappointment Mamma felt. We were disappointed, too, and we began to have another feeling that was painful — guilt. For we had always been on Daddy's side in the argument between them — an argument that was usually not stated but implied — that there was no need to worry about the future: everything would turn out all right. Suddenly that future was with us and it was turning out all wrong. Our friend, the lady from Nevada, had an expression that characterized the last year we spent in this town. She used to say glumly when more than one piece of bad luck followed another: "It never rains but what it pours." It poured all winter and on through the summer of the next year.

I took this inopportune time to grow taller and my winter coat of many years would no longer cover my skinny arms. We couldn't afford material for a new one so Mamma made me one out of two surplus World War I blankets. It wasn't a very beautiful color but it kept me warm. We had outgrown the overshoes we had at one time and had nothing but rubbers to wear in the snow. Mamma made leggings out of old coats that had been given to her, which buttoned up our legs with shoe buttons. They kept our legs warm when we first went out, but the snow got down into our shoes when we skied and we suffered from what people then called "chill blains" which, I suppose, was simply frost bite. When we came in from the cold we sat in front of the heater to warm our feet and they would begin to itch and be very painful. We tried a home remedy someone suggested — rubbing chalk on them — but it didn't do any good. We were often kept awake at night by our painful toes.

Mamma stretched what little money we had as far as it would go. There was no agency, no welfare office, we could go to for help. The poverty of our situation came home to me when on my birthday Mamma tried to make a cake without eggs and with very little sugar. It fell apart after it was baked and we had to eat it out of bowls.

Our last resource was to borrow money from relatives. This was a step I think Mamma hesitated to take because it was a tacit admission that Daddy had failed us, a circumstance that would not be a great surprise in her family. We saw her struggle painfully as she sat down to compose the humuliating requests. I am sure she always borrowed an insufficient amount in hopes that we would hear from Daddy, for we went on living on scanty rations. Another crisis faced us as spring came on: we were running out of fuel. We tried to stretch out the wood and coal we had until warm weather but we didn't quite make it. Sister and I went out on the hills behind the house and scrounged old boards from abandoned mines. When the snow was gone we went out with an axe and cut off dry sage brush but one of these expeditions ended badly when I fell on the axe and cut my leg. It was the kind of wound that should have been closed with stitches, but doctors were miles away and we had no money for such things. It healed satisfactorily but left a scar as a souvenir of that painful winter.

Even at school things went badly that year. The teacher was from a farming community in the valley and she didn't seem to understand mining town kids. She took a particular dislike to me and the feeling was mutual. At the end of the school year we wanted to put on a play but she vetoed the project. The class turned against her and we rehearsed the play ourselves and put it on in the Masonic Hall. It was a triumph for us but must have been a long evening for the audience as we struggled through our lines.

Misfortune kept "pouring" through our last summer in the town. We had two dogs — our faithful Shep, the "auld red faced thing," and a lively part airedale named Kelly, who had a long coat of buff colored hair which covered his face. Dogs as a rule ran free in Silver and although there were occasional dog fights no one paid much attention to them. One man had some hunting dogs which he kept confined in his yard. Kelly used to invade the dogs territory and set them barking furiously. One day the man who owned the dogs took his shot gun and shot Kelly as he ran away. The dog made it as far as our yard where he fell in a pool of blood. I ran up to him as he lay there dying and called his name. He wagged his tail weakly and died. We had learned from Daddy to be very fond of and sympathetic with animals. To see our beautiful lively dog die before our eyes in a pool of blood was a terrible blow to us. Mamma was so upset that she went right to the man's house (he was a near neighbor) and made him come and dispose of Kelly's body. Instead of burying it he threw it in the creek. Mamma went to the county officials and had him fined for polluting the creek. There were no laws governing the firing of guns within the town for there was no town government.

This incident was the last straw for us. Mamma knew that we had to leave before fall because we had finished grade school and if we were to have any further education we had to move. She asked one of her brothers to come and get us.

It was fortunate that we still did not own many things that would be hard to move. We gave away the toys that we had inherited from an earlier generation in Silver. The rest of our belongings fit in Mamma's trunk. The hardest part of our leave-taking was that we had to give away old Shep. Our Chinese friend Pete had always liked him and he agreed to keep him. For comfort we told ourselves that we would come back and get him someday.

We knew that we were leaving our childhood behind in this

town, but because of the miseries of the last year it wasn't a sad parting. We had visited Mamma's relatives in the valley and the life on the "outside" with its streetcars, movies, and automobiles, was an attractive prospect. We did not want to spend another year like the one we had just spent. The killing of our pet was a fresh wound, but there was a still deeper one. How could the father who had been such a joyous part of our lives go off and apparently forget us?

It was a good thing that we didn't know any more than we did about the situation in Mamma's family at that time. They were beginning to feel the pinch of competition from the chain stores which were moving into Idaho as the population increased. Up until that time her brothers had had a prosperous business in variety stores in five towns. All their stores were soon to go down in the face of that competition. And the great depression was only five years away. More poverty for us and for everyone was just around the corner.

But as we sped down the road that day in our uncle's car I think we were mainly happy because some kind of a solution to our problems seemed to be at hand. Maybe we had a few pangs as we passed the little stone powder houses, those uniquely mining-town structures, which had marked the limits of our forays from home on many happy expeditions.

CHAPTER XIII

SILVER MEETS A STRANGER

Eleven years later I was on my way back to Silver to show my home town to the man I was going to marry. Jim had lived in southern Idaho when he was a boy and he had always been curious about those mountains on the southern horizon. He had never heard anything about them in the farming community he lived in, but when he met me he began to hear plenty. Now as we drove across the sagebrush hills out of Murphy I began to have misgivings about the wonders I had described. Were the mountains really as steep and impressive as I had led Jim to believe? He had worked one summer in the Selway-Locksa area where he had come face to face with bears on forest trails and he had often described to me the beauty of the Selway River and Selway Falls. Did I really have anything to show him in this dry desert country to compare with that? As we churned up the dust of the one-lane road in an old Dodge roadster, wound down Whiskey Hill into Sinker Canyon, and followed the road up the canyon with the mountains completely shut out from our view (the road today does not follow the same course) I began to wonder if my childhood memories hadn't made everything bigger and grander than it was. At last we broke out of the canyon and began to follow a small stream lined with cottonwoods and sage brush. A few juniper trees dotted the steep sides of the bare hills as we climbed further. I spotted a mahogany tree and we stopped to look at it because Jim was not familiar with the shrub although he had had a year's training in forestry. We discovered when we stopped that the water in the car's radiator was boiling but we urged it on to a spot I remembered which had once been a stage station where we could pull off the road. We hadn't met a car yet but on this one-lane road with sharp turns it was not safe where there was no turn-out. When we came to the old station buildings we were within sight of War Eagle Mountain. It was still patched with snow and several of the old mines were visible from this point. But Jim was too preoccupied with the boiling radiator to pay much attention to the scenery. He wondered if there was much of a climb ahead of us. I told him that as I remembered it we were about to start the long climb to the summit. When the car had cooled enough so we could add water to the radiator we went on. Around the next turn we started up a steep grade and now as we left the plains and canyons behind us I could see that I had not exaggerated: the mountains were as steep and rugged and beautiful as I remembered them. Jim was busy straddling high centers and coaxing the old Dodge, whose tires were worn smooth, over patches of bedrock, so I didn't insist that he notice and comment on the scene. The road in 1936, two years after the citizens of Owyhee County had voted to move the county seat away from Silver, looked as if a decision had been made to abandon it. Little streams were eating away at it and in places it looked more like a path than a road. At last we entered the welcome shade of firs, rounded Cottonwood Turn, and came out on the summit. We got out and looked back at the layers of mountains and hills and volcanic bluffs, river valleys and more mountains beyond. Then we turned and looked the other way at the mine-scarred mountains rising from the bed of Jordan Creek. "My God!" Jim said. "What a country!"

As we wound down the road toward the creek we passed through thickets of mahogany, patches of aspen with their tiny new leaves trembling in the breeze, firs, junipers, and everywhere huge granite rocks. A bouquet of wonderful fragrances on the clear, bracing, air brought more exclamations from Jim. All my rosy memories were completely vindicated.

We started up the hill in front of the Idaho Hotel, but the Dodge figured it had had enough, coughed and died. We rolled back down to the bridge and tried again. This time we made it and pulled up in front of the Courthouse. The offices of the building were dark. There was no one on the streets. We drove over to the Idaho Power sub-station and found our friend Ben Kidder. He invited us to stay for the night and filled us in on former residents. Old Pete was dead and he had a story to tell about him. He had been helping dismantle the Catholic Church when it became a menace to other buildings. Ben had been out of town and when he came back he found Pete with his hand swathed in bandages. What had happened, Ben asked. "Tear down Jees Clist's house," Pete said. And then nodding wisely and holding up his injured hand. "Smash thumb." That was what you might expect, he meant, if you did something displeasing to the deities. It sounded as if that "nice fella" had turned into a Chinese god.

Our old Shep, Ben told us, had been killed by a car in front of Pete's store. We remarked on the empty streets and Ben said there were not many people around since the Courthouse closed. Judge Leonard hadn't moved down to Murphy and he was on call if he was needed. That gave us an idea. We were planning on being married in June. Why not come back here and be married in my home town?

I saw a few more old friends that day and I learned that many I knew were dead. Mike Rock had died shortly after we left Silver. The old timers were thinning out. I was surprised when I rounded a corner and almost collided with Rudy. He was standing firm as a rock as usual. I had to tell him who I was and when he finally understood he showered me with some of his choice expletives. I asked about Anna and he swelled with pride as he told me that she was married and had five sons. "She no make no girls, Anna," he assured me proudly. In his old country view, the next best thing to being a man was to produce them.

We visited with Will Hawes who became the last permanent resident of Silver for many years. His nephew, Fred Leonard, was staying with him and they were still keeping the little store Will's father Richard Hawes had operated for years. "Dickie," as we called him had migrated to the United States from Cornwall in 1866, going first to the mines in New Jersey and Connecticut, and then setting sail for California where he worked in the boom town of Grass Valley. He lived in Fairview for a while and Will was born there. He kept a store in Delamar where his daughter Lillie who became Judge Leonard's wife was born. The Leonards raised a large family in Silver, some of whom were my school mates. Their children and grandchildren are among the faithful former townspeople who go back in the summer.

Jim and I got our marriage license in Murphy in June of that year and were married by Judge Leonard in his office in the Courthouse. Ben Kidder and Eleanor Lewis, a childhood friend, were our witnesses. We were the next to the last couple to be married in that historic building.

CHAPTER XIV

THE CHALLENGE ON THE MOUNTAIN

We didn't expect to have much contact with Silver after our marriage but three months later we found ourselves living in a cabin on War Eagle Mountain where my father had a contract to run a tunnel in the direction of a shaft on the Oro Grande property. Jim had lost his job on a federally funded highway project when it ran out of funds — a common happening in the Depression — and Daddy had come to the rescue. He needed a mucker and a cook and although neither Jim nor I could claim experience in those lines he took us on. My job didn't call for any remuneration. Daddy assumed that I would want to be with Jim and he counted on my known partiality for the Owyhee mountains as another drawing card. And it never occurred to me that my efforts to put three meals on the table, to keep a fire going in the range, to carry water from a stream for cooking and washing, to keep the cabin clean, might have commanded a wage.

One other attraction our employment held for Daddy was that we had a car and he didn't. Our old Dodge roadster would take us to the mine and provide transportation after we were there, for a while, at least, until the snow came. It couldn't carry the supplies and food we would need for three or more months so Daddy hired a man with a truck to bring up a load of dynamite, fuse, caps, carbide, and a supply of groceries. Jim and I were delegated to buy the food. We tried to get Daddy to help us out with a list but every time we mentioned the subject he would say: "Let's see, we'll need —" and he'd spread his big hand and start counting on his fingers. "Powder, fuse, caps, and carbide." Then he'd look off into the distance, seeing himself already engaged in his favorite occupation — working underground. Finally we decided that we couldn't get him to consider anything so mundane as food so we went to a grocery store and threw the manager into a panic by telling him we wanted to buy three month's groceries for three people all in one shot. It wasn't often in those days that a customer came into a store to spend such a large sum on food.

We adjusted quickly to the primitive conditions at the mine. Eating supper by the light of an oil lamp and heating water on the range soon became a way of life. My father wasn't daunted by the lack of power for the mine, depending, as he had so often in the past, on the strength of his muscles. He had to drill the holes for the dynamite by hand and it was a matter of pride with him to "get the round in," — that is, to drill eight or ten holes in the solid granite face of the tunnel every day. Jim was not used to the back-breaking labor of mucking out the pile of shattered rock and earth left by the explosions but he managed to get it done in time for the next day's "round" by working after supper. The owner of the mine had built a small blacksmith shop and supplied it with tools and fuel so the "steel," as the drills are called, could be sharpened daily. This was a task that often took Daddy back to the mine after the evening meal.

I had to keep the food hot for an indefinite period because of delays at the mine. Some rock is harder than others and occasionally Daddy had to come out and sharpen steel before he could finish the round. The cabin was across a draw from the mine and when at last I saw their carbide lights on the dump I knew that it was time for the exploding dynamite to mark the hour for supper. This was the crisis time of day. I watched and counted with them. The first shots rang out loud and clear and sent the dog scurrying under the bed. We waited with hope and fear for the last ones — "the lifters" — which made a muffled "pouff" as they exploded under the mass of shattered rock blown out from the ones above. There is nothing a miner dreads more than a missed hole, for the live cap is still there somewhere in the pile of muck and the single stroke of a shovel or pick could set it off. When one of the charges failed to go off Daddy always went in by himself after supper and looked for the fuse and cap. If all the shots went off Daddy would give one of his great whoops of joy, the dog would come out of hiding, and we would sit down to supper in good spirits after the tense moment of counting.

If Jim finished his mucking chores the night before or was able to get it done early the next day we were free to go down to Silver to pick up the mail. We missed being cut off from the news of the world especially the political news of that year of 1936. We didn't have a radio at the mine but we could listen to the news for a few minutes in one of the stores in town. The stage still went in and out every day but the town was only a shadow of itself as it had been when the courthouse was occupied. The hotel was closed, too, except for a small attached building on one end which had been the barroom. A man who was new to the town sold bottled beer there legally and stronger stuff illegally upon request. He was a friendly, talkative, man who was called Tip by everyone in town. I never found out his real name. He had another business, too, in the old telephone office where he lived. He had brought with him from a town in the valley the remains of a second hand store and he sometimes sold some of the articles from it to tourists as souvernirs of Silver City.

When we came to town Tip, who was obviously lonesome for company, used to follow us around on our errands as if everything we did was of intense interest to him. Finally when we showed signs of having finished our mission he'd say: "Well, I'll go down and open up." The eager look in his eyes told us that he would be immensely disappointed if we didn't stop at the barroom. We were always amused by a little ceremony he performed after he unlocked the door. He'd go around the bar and remove a worn cigar box from a little drawer, take a comb out of the box and carefully part and comb his hair in front of the bar's mirror. Then he'd turn to us and say: "What'll ya have?" He seemed to enjoy his role of bartender so much that I wondered if he could be fulfilling some kind of boyhood dream, perhaps inspired by Western stories, by serving customers in this historic spot. If he had come here to make a fortune he was surely in the wrong place at the wrong time.

The fall season was long and beautiful that year. But as the dry snowless days stretched on into November our little stream dried up and we had to find a new source of water. Daddy refused to consider the problem for a long time although Jim and I mentioned it frequently. He couldn't believe that there were any serious problems as long as things were going well at the mine. But one evening when he came into the cabin he found the water pail empty. "What am I going to do for drinking water?" He demanded, as if Jim and I had no such needs. He was finally compelled to address the problem and he guided us up the steep hillside to the lower Oro Fino tunnel, one of the very first mines on the mountain. A clear stream of water ran from a seam at the mouth of the tunnel. It was a steep climb from the cabin to our new source of water and it was evident even to Daddy that I couldn't descend it with a water bucket in each hand. So Jim was excused to fetch water twice a day, much to the delight of the dog who seemed to think that the trip was undertaken for his benefit. I carried the teakettle, for every drop we brought back filled some need. Jim was always happy to get out of the mine for a while and enjoy the fine fresh air. Before long another opportunity to enjoy working in the open presented itself, one that my father considered more than just a run of bad luck: to him it was a real tragedy when they hit soft ground in a fault in the mine. Drilling, of course, was easier, but the tunnel kept collapsing dangerously around them. There was nothing to do but timber it up.

Since there were no timbers lying around at this mine to be put in place, they had to go out on the hillside and cut down trees. From the lower parts of the tree they fashioned timbers and cross pieces to place over them. The upper slender parts they used for "lagging" — the poles laid from timber to timber which made a ceiling for the tunnel. Daddy fretted about the loss of time, for he was being paid by the foot and the sooner he reached the shaft the less his expense would be. But more than that he simply hated to be out of the mine.

I used to carry their lunch to the spot about a quarter of a mile from the cabin where they were cutting timber. We would sit on the bank of the road enjoying the sunshine and the smell of the freshly cut trees as we ate. One day Jim and I were sitting there waiting for Daddy to finish trimming a log. Jim had just finished rhapsodizing about how wonderful it was to be out here in the sunshine and fresh air, when Daddy came climbing up toward us wiping his face on his sleeve and cursing to himself. "God," he said earnestly. "I'll be glad to get down in the mine again. This sunshine is killing me!" He was puzzled when we laughed at him. "I mean it!" He shouted indignantly.

We knew the wonderful fall weather couldn't last forever so one day Jim and I took our old car down the mountain to the main road into Silver and put it in a shed at an old stage station. This part of the road was directly below the mine. Before we left, Daddy showed us how we could climb back up the mountain by an old road used in the early days. It was now nothing more than a faint path, and it was so steep that it was hard to believe it had ever been used as a road. As we were climbing back up I found what I thought was a broken horseshoe, but it was strangely shaped with a wide part at one end. I decided to keep it and ask Daddy about it when we got back to the mine. "It's a bull shoe," he told me. "Or half of one, that is. They hauled supplies up that road by ox team in the early days and they hauled ore down it to a mill, too." I kept it as a souvenir of the early days and now it is a memento of our days at the mine.

The good weather held out until the very last days of November as it sometimes does in these mountains. But what we had long expected greeted our eyes one morning — a curtain of snow flakes so thick we couldn't see the mine dump across the gulch. Daddy once again used the weather to vindicate his opinion about the superiority of working underground. "Now, Jim," he said. "Ain't it a good thing we've got a nice dry place to work over there in the tunnel?"

We knew now that it was unlikely that we would be making any more trips into Silver and we would probably have no more company at the mine but our own. We hadn't been inundated with visitors before the weather changed. The mine owner dropped in occasionally and once a passing sheep herder brought us a leg of lamb. The road to this mine branched off the road from Silver to War Eagle Mountain so we didn't even see other miners who were working there. We could see this road far above us as it made a turn and we could also see a small piece of the main road into Silver far below us. The cabin sat on a ledge of rock below two towering peaks and it overlooked a sheer drop-off into a gulch. Sometimes when it was raining in the valleys the clouds would fill the gulch below us and give us the feeling that we were suspended in space. It was an isolated spot and after the snow came we realized more than ever that we were on our own, out of touch with even the shrunken town of Silver.

The snow had solved one problem for us, though. We now had water at hand and we had all the vessels we could find, even rusty cans salvaged from a former mining venture, which we filled with snow and left to melt in the cabin. We learned the bitter lesson of how little water content snow can have, but this was our only recourse now, for the path down the mountain from the old tunnel was too steep to negotiate in the snow. Our diet was beginning to lack the variety it had at the beginning of our stay. We had been a little too lavish with our use of dried fruits and canned vegetables and the only meat we had left was the remains of a huge ham. We still had macaroni and a piece of what had once been a wheel of cheese. The question was could I make the food last until Daddy and Jim broke through to the shaft? I began stretching the ham out with casserole dishes, saving the fat for the food of last resort — a sack of beans. We had a can of cocoa and a little sugar. When Daddy complained of being hungry after supper I made cups of hot cocoa. We had brought a sack of flour and some dry yeast with which I began making our bread, a skill that

Julia Welch at the mine, 1936.

required much experimenting and the capacity to absorb a lot of teasing from Daddy. At the end of our stay we had to content ourselves with my rather heavy bread and boiled beans.

One morning as I was clearing away the remains of a scanty breakfast, Daddy and Jim burst through the door of the cabin bringing the gusts of a blizzard with them — and great news: they had broken through to the shaft with last night's round. All they had to do now was muck out and shape up the tunnel a little. By the time they

Jim Welch at the mine, 1936.

Leaving the mine, 1936.

got that done, Daddy said, the blizzard would be over and we would head for the valley.

The weather didn't cooperate for a few days. We existed on our monotonous diet and played cards by lamp light. We remembered suddenly that we had our clothes and bedding to take out with us. It would be hard to manage the steep trip down the slope carrying suit-cases and bedrolls. Daddy remembered a piece of tin he'd seen near the mine. He retrieved it, and it formed the bottom of a tobaggan he made to hold our gear.

When the break in the weather came we tied our belongings to the tobaggan, not forgetting the remains of the beans and flour for nothing was thrown away in those times, and got ready to go down the mountain. It was a bright cold morning when we left. Jim took a picture of me with the dog in the snow and another one of Daddy and me with the tobaggan.

I have always been reluctant to leave any place I've lived in, feel-ing as if I am leaving a part of my life there. Leaving this crude little cabin was no exception. But as we started out to find the old road, my gloom was soon erased by the dog's antics as he bounded through the snow, convinced, as usual that this expedition was in his honor. He would race ahead and then come back to express his jubilation by jumping on us and knocking us flat in the snow. We laughed at each other's mishaps, my father's voice ringing out in the great empty ex-panse of mountain and gulch, as we slid and tumbled down the steep hill where the pioneer miners with ox-teams had struggled up seven-ty years before.

We had lived at the mine during those months under conditions that were very like those the pioneers lived under. Our cabin had been as crude and bare of comforts as the early ones and Daddy and Jim had worked the mine with exactly the same methods the early miner used. Our jubilant mood as we made our way down the moun-tain that morning was partly due, I think, to the fact that we felt as many of the pioneers must have felt at times — that we had met the challenge of time and nature and we had won.

CHAPTER XV

GOING BACK

We had mixed feelings about going back to Silver after World War II. We knew that the Courthouse had been torn down and we heard rumors about vandalism and ransacking of buildings. But in the end the attraction of the mountains as part of our past was too much for us and in 1947 we set out on the familiar road up Rabbit Creek in the first new car we had ever owned. The trip from Murphy had always been a rather rough one, but now it looked as if we were on a road that had been abandoned for years. Little streams had eaten gullies so deep that our bumper and tail pipes grated as we eased through them. High centers threatened the car's undersides and, as we crept up the canyon toward the mountains, overgrown willows and choke cherry bushes clawed at its new paint. Our progress was so slow that the car overheated and we had to stop before we began the climb to the summit.

We pulled off the road at the site of the stage station where we had left the Dodge when we were at the mine. We could see the side of War Eagle Mountain where we had tumbled down with our homemade tobaggan eleven years ago. The air here was fresh and cool, so refreshing after the heat of the desert, and in spite of the damage to our new car we began to feel the exhilaration that the trip always inspired.

But after we crossed the summit and crept up the last steep rise into town our mood changed abruptly. The destruction of the heart of the town had been pretty complete. Only the stone arches of the Courthouse stood among the rubble of its rock foundation. The old saloon buildings and the big general store buildings had been razed. Broken glass glittered in the dust, much of it the kind of old glass that turns amethyst under the sun. Papers from the files of the Courthouse blew about the streets. I began picking them up and reading the familiar names until my eyes blurred with tears. Everywhere I looked I saw something that was part of my past, torn and scattered. Even the old foot bridge across the creek was gone.

Further up the street I saw the effects of a fire that had leveled several buildings in the intervening years. It had started in an old stone building with an iron roof and iron doors which had once belonged to Sam Heidleberger. When we lived in Silver it was used as a storehouse by C. M. Caldwell who owned the general store at that time. The cause of the fire was thought to be spontaneous combustion of something stored in it. Will Hawes told us that the heat of that fire was unbelievable. It burned three houses on the hill behind it, one of them Judge Leonard's house. If anyone had asked me what building in town was most likely to survive a fire I would have pointed to Sam Heidelberger's building. Some of its old stone walls are still standing. It was a wonder that the whole town didn't go.

During the war the town and the mines around it were stripped of anything made of iron. Before this time many of the old mills were still intact. Now if they are even standing they are just hollow shells. I don't know how much of the scrounging was authorized but I have a suspicion that many buildings were torn down without permission and iron stripped from mines whose owners were far away. Private houses were ransacked for antiques, windows were broken by vandals. A man in the valley said to my husband that he understood that you could go up to Silver and take anything you wanted from the houses. "You could," Jim said coldly. "But it would be stealing."

The schoolhouse, the Masonic Hall, and the hotel were still intact, as were the Avalanche Office, the Telephone Office and the Post Office. It was the last year for the town as an official Post Office. Will Hawes was the only year round resident and he would continue to live there for close to twenty years.

Jim and I were depressed by the destruction around us. He had just come back from overseas where he had seen too many similar scenes. We decided to hike to the top of Florida Mountain. It was more of a hike than I remembered., although I did recall that the "top" you see from town is not the real top. As you go up, the mountain grows, and the real top appears. We stopped near the false top at an old tunnel which has ice in it all year and again at an old mine dump visible from town with an old mine building on it. On the real top we were rewarded with a spectacular view of mountains, valleys, creek beds, and deserts to the west. As I looked at the summits and gulches around us I knew that I would always come back here even if all the town disappeared.

Six years later when our children were six and seven years old we started going back to Silver again. We rented a house above the town near the old Potosi Mine. Mrs. Leonard was there for the summer with Will, running the little store their father had kept. She told me she missed being up on the hill in the house which had burned. It was just below the house we were living in. "You can see everything that happens in town from up there," she said regretfully. "Everything" wasn't much nowadays, but the town was coming back as a summer place. People had started fixing up old houses and Will was often called upon to help trace an old water line or patch a broken pipe.

I often stopped in at the store to talk to Mrs. Leonard. She was a lively, gracious, little lady and a living repository of the names of people who had once lived in the town. I would point out a house to her and say: "Now who lived there? I can't remember."

"That's where Winchesters lived," she'd say. And then she looked annoyed with herself for making such a mistake and say: "But heavens, what's the matter with me! That was before your time. I'll tell you who lived there! Do you remember Mrs. Simon Harris? Why, of course you do! You and Adelaide (her daughter) were in some of those programs she put on during the War. You marched around holding little flags and sang!" And she would laugh at that happy memory.

The things she told me started some remembrances on my part. Simon Harris! I hadn't thought of him for years. His was the first funeral I ever attended. He was an important man in town because he had long held offices in the miners' union. I remember being part of what to me was a very large crowd in the Masonic Hall. Simon was a Mason of long standing and the funeral was conducted with all the robes and rituals of the Lodge. Since I had never attended a funeral I didn't know what to expect, and I looked around for Simon Harris who was now dead. I decided that he was the man in the big chair with a strange hat on his head. But presently we joined a line of people who were marching around the room and I noticed for the first time that there was a rather long box sitting on the floor. I stood on tip-toe to look into it and there was Simon Harris. Strangely enough I still held on to my first impression even though I went to the cemetery and saw the box put into the ground. That night I dreamed that the man in the chair with his peculiar hat and robes was being lowered into a hole with much difficulty.

Another former townsman who had come back was Tom Rock. He had opened a little bar in an old building of his father's across from the Hotel. I spent some time talking to him, too, and enjoyed his flair for telling stories. We had in common our Irish background and an interest in the peculiarities of speech we heard as children. Tom was an excellent mimic and in addition he had that love of telling a story which is apparent in much of Irish literature. When he told stories about his father he entered Mike's character and at times I could swear that it was Mike leaning against his post in front of the Sheriff's office holding court to an audience.

One day I mentioned to him that his father had helped people out when they were hard up. "Yes," Tom said with some bitterness. "He was good to everybody but his own family. Why, if Mamma asked for five dollars he'd go white as a sheet!"

We renewed acquaintance with the Ned Williams family during those summers. Ned's wife Floribel, who had grown up at her father's mine north of Silver, took us on jaunts up mountain roads in her Jeep. We went far up Long Gulch beyond the Blaine and Banner Mines to a spot where Indians had camped long ago and made arrow heads out of obsidian. We found some points in good condition and many scraps and discarded broken ones. Visiting the former campsite brought memories of the Indians who used to come to Silver every summer or fall from the Duck Valley Reservation which is half in Owyhee County and half in Nevada. They set up their tents and wagons on the ball grounds on the side of Florida Mountain. We could see their bright blankets from across the creek when we lived in the little house behind the school house. Two old women known as Susie and Maggie used to go around town begging. I remember one contact I had with one of them when we lived in Sam Heidelberger's house, the year I started to school. I was playing in the dirt behind the house when I looked up and saw an Indian woman looking down at me. In spite of the stories I had heard about Indians I was not afraid, and when she told me to go ask my mother to give her something I took it upon myself to decide on the gift. Maybe just at that moment I had been thinking of a box of fresh Italian prunes Mamma had bought from a peddler and stored in a little cellar under the house. I went down the cellar steps and got two handsful of prunes and presented them to her. Mamma came out just as I presented them and the Indian woman held them out, laughing and saying: "She gave me these." Mamma laughed, too, and went in the house and came back with some coins. They laughed some more while I stood trying to figure out why my gift was funny.

After those summers in the '50's we moved out of the State and did not come back to Silver for twelve years. In the 60's we came back with a camper and pulled a little Volkswagon behind it for going up on the old mine roads. The old town had gone through more changes and the old timers were being replaced by new people.

Tom Rock died in 1966 and Will Hawes in 1968. Mrs. Leonard continued to keep the little store in summers and Tom's wife Lillian ran the little bar across from the hotel for a few years. These two and the Ned Williams family were often the only people we saw in town

The empty streets of Silver City in the 1950s.

from the old days. By 1970 both Lillian Rock and Mrs. Leonard were gone.

Many of those we saw in town in summers were young people who were enjoying living in an historic, isolated, spot, close to nature. They were also, I think, enjoying the simple life without the amenities of a civilization they had come to look down on during the days of the Viet Nam War. To them living here was a kind of protest. I think the way I felt about this new population was somewhat the way a real milk maid must have felt about Marie Antoinette's playing milk maid at Trianon. I felt patronized. Another thing that bothered me was that these new people were creating myths about what had happened in the past. It is always a temptation to make a story a little better in the telling: I've succumbed to it myself. But it bothered me that every day the past got more violent in the telling, the ore got richer, the past population larger. A new town was being created. I should have looked at it as a passing phase that would soon die out. It did. And I am now rather ashamed of how I felt. After all I didn't have any valid claim on the place. I didn't even own property in it and when I was growing up there my family was one of a group known as "Johnnie Come Latelies" — an expression used by the old families who felt threatened, as people always do, by new blood. Daddy had come to the County in the '90's (we could never pin him down on a date) and Mamma in the early nineteen hundreds. I don't know when the cut-off date was for a person to be called a "Johnnie Come Lately" but I knew that we were not of the exclusive club of old timers. And yet here I was resenting someone's innocent enjoyment of "my" territory!

Every year as we drove around the mountain roads the place seemed more beautiful to me. As a matter of fact it actually was, for when trees and shrubs were no longer needed for wood to get people through those cold winters, a wonderful new crop of Alpine firs pierced the skies again, and the mahogany and junipers, rabbit brush and sage, were beginning to hide the scars of mining. Herds of deer hid in the thick brush on Florida Mountain. Snowshoe hare and sage hens could be seen on War Eagle. Eagles nested in high outcrops, and the mountain bluebird, Idaho's state bird, fluttered from bush to bush along the sides of seldom traveled gulches. The countryside was very familiar to us and yet always capable of treating us to some surprise — a bird that was new to us, a plant we hadn't noticed before, or an old scene looking new because of different lighting.

We spent the rainiest August on record in Idaho camped beside Jordan Creek. Many of the summer people left town until finally we and Mrs. Leonard were the only ones left. We stopped to see her every day and always found her hopeful that the next day would be bright again. It was still raining when Jim's vacation was over and we had to leave. But even those rainy days had their compensations. Sitting in the camper we saw birds in the willows we had never seen before — little flycatchers puffed up against the chill and thrushes hopping along the creek under the protection of the leaves.

It wasn't just enjoyment of nature that brought me back here, though. For me it was a place where the past was still alive. Even the buildings that were gone evoked a memory when I walked past their former sites. I couldn't pass the spot where the livery stable stood on Jordan Street without remembering Jack Hunt and his little room full of calendars, and the horses stamping in their stalls. And the windows of the house where the pioneer lady from New York kept her bright geraniums brought back the memory of those happy visits. On the hotel porch I could still see the old miners who used to sit there in good weather talking in low voices, waiting for the stir of activity when the stage arrived. At night they walked back to their little shacks, built a fire, and cooked their supper. Like my father and many others in town they had come here with high hopes. Now they sat and waited and talked over the mines they had worked in, level by level.

The town, the mountains, and the mines provided another dimension of enjoyment when I started reading and collecting materials about its past. Now I knew the stories behind some of the names on the tombstones, I knew of the incidents that gave Dead Man's Alley its name, I knew who had owned some of the mines, and the struggles that went on over ownership of the twisted ledges of War Eagle Mountain. On the east side of the gulch in town I could see the foundation stones of the old courthouse of territorial days which burned in the '80's when a white man, indignant at being locked up with a Chinese, set his bed afire. Both men died in the fire.

I knew from reading the death notices in old copies of the Avalanche that the tombstones didn't tell the whole story of death and disappointment in this place. Many others were buried in these cemeteries who were not commemorated in marble. Some died in mine accidents, some froze to death in blizzards, some were killed by avalanches, some committed suicide. Women died in childbirth, children died of contagious diseases. Like the old men who sat on the hotel porch in my childhood, these people joined the great body of anonymous actors in the drama of the past.

Just as my remembrances of this place were both good and bad, so was its history. The newspaper told of parties, dances, school entertainments, lecturers and traveling troupes, horse races, ball games, drilling contests, big Fourth of July celebrations. It was like many another small town in the United States. And yet it was unique. People came here to look at it, to wonder about it, to learn about it. Why?

I think part of its attraction is the glamourization of the West that occurred as civilization pushed its way across the Mississippi. These little mining towns whose gold had given out were like Pompei — they were preserved from progress by an act of nature. People came to see them because they hadn't gone on growing and developing like the towns they were used to; time had stopped here and they could witness it. And then there is an aura which draws people to places where gold and silver are found. The shiny stuff has long decorated the ornaments of leaders as far back as the secret of metal working became known. It is "magic" stuff. Then, too, many people subscribe to the legends about the finding of gold, of how somebody's obliging burro pawed up a wonderful ledge at the very moment when his master sat with his head in his hands, bemoaning his fate. The prospector will very likely have little capital in addition to the burro and if he doesn't know where to go to find it he can do nothing about his rich strike. So he sells his claim for the best offer he can get and goes away thinking he is rich. Henry Comstock sold the richest claims in the West in Virginia City for $11,000. It must have seemed like a fortune to him. He went off prospecting and came back to Virginia before long, broke. He took off for Montana then, where he committed suicide.

The purchasers of the prospectors' claims either have money or know where to get it and they are the ones who take out the millions which add more luster to the story of mining. The people who come to old mining towns want to be amazed by the legend of the lowly prospector who found a fortune. They have probably had to work hard for the money they've earned and they like to hear about serendipitous happenings — buried treasure, big winnings at the gaming tables, chance discoveries of gold and silver and even lead. (Noah Kellogg's burro is supposed to have pawed up the big North Idaho Bunker Hill ledges of lead and silver.) Ghost towns are sad places — places where lots of hopes died. But the legends about them are dazzling.

When my father came to the prosperous town of Silver City in the '90's he must have been dazzled by the tales he heard of the wonderful mines on War Eagle Mountain in the '60's. At the time he arrived the town was prosperous because of later discoveries on Florida Mountain opposite War Eagle, and mines further down the creek at Dewey, Blackjack, and Delamar. He prospected and staked claims on War Eagle and worked for wages in the mines to finance more prospecting. He made a mistake when he got married and started a family. He was used to the freedom of a bachelor's life. It didn't matter if he quit a job and went off prospecting when he had only himself to worry about. He had kindly feelings toward most people and great sympathy for the underdog. He didn't care a fig for money although he was supposedly seeking a fortune. If he had money he didn't begrudge spending it on us. But he never really assumed the burden of providing for a family.

At one time I could have said of him as Tom said of his father: "He was good to everybody but his own family." But as I got older I began to realize that although he had failed us as a provider, he had given us attitudes that shaped our lives. His sympathy for the unfortunate, his interest in the world about him and beyond it to the planets and stars, his questioning of propositions that other people took for granted — all this rubbed off on us.

After we moved to Boise Mamma found out that he was in Boise Basin working at different mines and doing a little prospecting on the side. We saw him infrequently when he came to Boise. Mamma worked and assumed the burden of providing for us when we went to High School. I had won some prizes for writing from a magazine published for high school students. With this money and some I had earned during the summer I went to the University. My sister stayed in Boise, married and raised a family.

Daddy had changed his scene of operations to another mining district — Atlanta, Idaho — when he was seriously injured. This community was like Silver in its isolation in the winter time, but a plane managed to land there and bring him out to the hospital in Boise. Mamma and Sister were most solicitous in their support of him. He recovered from most of his injuries, but the sight of one eye was nearly gone. In spite of this, he went back to the mines when he recovered. Mamma became ill shortly after this with arthritis. After I was married they went off to some mines together as they had in the old days before Sister and I were born. Mamma did the cooking and Daddy worked in mines in Pine, Idaho, Yellow Pine, and even on War Eagle Mountain in Silver. Mamma enjoyed being in mining country again and in spite of all that had happened she was genuinely fond of my father. After a rather long stay at an antimony mine outside of Yellow Pine they came back to Boise, bought a small acreage, and built a house with the help of Jim. Mamma died in 1948, Daddy ten years later. Those last years without her were hard on him and I think he came at last to appreciate her love and support as he moved around from place to place, never content in any spot. Another tragedy overtook him when he lost the sight of his good eye and had only minimal sight in the damaged one.

Once when I was talking to Tom Rock in Silver in the '60's he told me about seeing Daddy up there not too long before he died. He had come up with some men from Boise who wanted to look at a mine he had told them about. He couldn't see well enough to walk around so they left him in Tom's bar while they went up on the mountain. He sat and talked to Tom for a while and then got restless and decided to walk around a bit. Tom helped him down the steps and stood watching him as he walked up the street.

"I saw this other old fellow coming toward Chris," Tom said. "He walked right up to him until his face was right in front of Chris's and said something." Tom started to laugh. "My God! All hell broke loose! Chris gave one of his big howls and started shouting: 'Andy Swan! Andy Swan!' They really kicked up the dust out there! I guess they thought they'd never see each other again and here they were, face to face, the only ones on the street. The two old prospectors! I wish you could have seen 'em."

I could see them all right, meeting in that silent, empty, ruined town. They had known it when the saloons stayed open all night to accommodate the men coming off shift, when stamp mills shook the old wooden buildings, when teams and wagons brought in supplies, when ore wagons rumbled down the gulches. It was all gone. I could see the backdrop of their meeting, too — that old mountain, War Eagle, its scars healing over, still keeping its secrets, enduring after all the struggle for its riches was over. It had nourished their hopes for years and now it was the grave of their dreams.

NOTES

Chapter I

[1] *A Historical, Descriptive and Commercial Directory of Owyhee County, Idaho:* Press of the Owyhee Avalanche, 1898.

Chapter X

[1] Report of the preliminary hearing for F. A. Young in the records of the Owyhee County Courthouse, Murphy, Idaho
[2] Idaho Daily Statesman, Boise, Idaho, June 15 and 17, 1921.
[3] Owyhee Avalanche, Silver City, Idaho, June 12 1921.
[4] Idaho Daily Statesman, Boise, Idaho, May 8, 1922.
[5] The Evening Capital News, Boise, Idaho, May 8, 1922.
[6] Owyhee Avalanche, Silver City, Idaho, May 12, 1922.